Ordnance Survey

The
Yorkshire Dales
and York

Landranger Guidebook

JARROLD

How to use this Guide

Pre-planning:
First look at the KEY MAP section — this shows the area covered, the towns and villages, and the starting point for the 12 Walks and 10 Tours. If you are unfamiliar with the area, look up some of the towns and villages in the PLACES OF INTEREST section. The WALKS or TOURS will provide further local information. The introductions will give you a feeling for the history, landscape, and wildlife of the area.

On the Spot:
From your chosen base, explore the area by road or on foot. Stars (★) after a place name indicate that it is featured in the PLACES OF INTEREST section (this is necessary as it is not possible to include every village and town because of space limitations). Some 28 places of interest are accompanied by maps to enable you to plan a short stroll. The scale of these is 2¹/₂ INCHES to 1 MILE (see CONVENTIONAL SIGNS for rights of way etc).

Landranger Maps:
These are the natural companions to the Guide. Places of interest are identified first with the number of the Landranger Map on which it appears (sometimes more than one). This is followed by two letters indicating the National Grid Square and by a 4-figure reference number. To locate any place or feature referred to on the relevant Landranger map, first read the two figures along the north or south edges of the map, then the two figures along the east or west edges. Trace the lines adjacent to each of the two sets of figures across the map face, and the point where they intersect will be the south-west corner of the grid square in which the place or feature lies.

Acknowledgements

We should like to thank those individuals and organisations who helped in the preparation of this book: Anthony Burton who, with assistance from Pip Burton, chose the walks and tours, suggested the photographic selection, and compiled and wrote the text; the National Park Officer of the Yorkshire Dales National Park; the Yorkshire and Humberside Tourist Board; Peter Titchmarsh for reading and commenting upon the text; Paula Chasty for the artwork; Curtis Garratt Limited for editing, designing, and typesetting the guide.

First published 1989 by Ordnance Survey and Jarrold Colour Publications

Ordnance Survey
Romsey Road
Maybush
Southampton SO9 4DH

Jarrold Colour
Publications
Barrack Street
Norwich NR3 1TR

Printed in Great Britain by Jarrold and Sons Ltd. Norwich

Contents

Key Maps   4

Introduction   8

The Natural History of the Dales   19

Leisure Activities — Useful addresses
and telephone numbers   28

Places of Interest   32

Motor and Cycle Tours   86

Walks in the Dales   106

Conventional Signs   132

Maps and Mapping   135

Index   138

KEY MAP INDEX

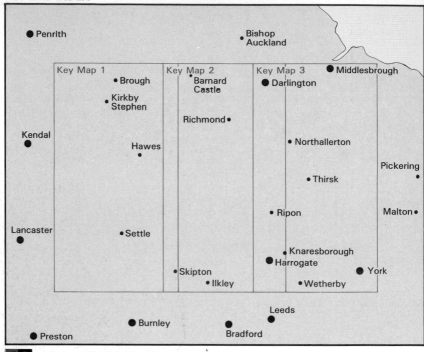

● Penrith

Bishop
Auckland

Key Map 1   Key Map 2   Key Map 3   ● Middlesbrough

● Brough   Barnard   ● Darlington
Castle

● Kirkby
Stephen

Richmond ●

Kendal

Hawes   ● Northallerton
●

● Thirsk   Pickering
●

● Ripon   Malton ●

Lancaster
●

● Settle   ● Knaresborough
Harrogate

● Skipton   ● York

● Ilkley   ● Wetherby

Leeds
●

● Burnley

Bradford

● Preston

2 Motor and Cycle Tour Start

1 Walk Start

Mini-Walk Start

LANDRANGER MAPS OF YORK AND THE DALES

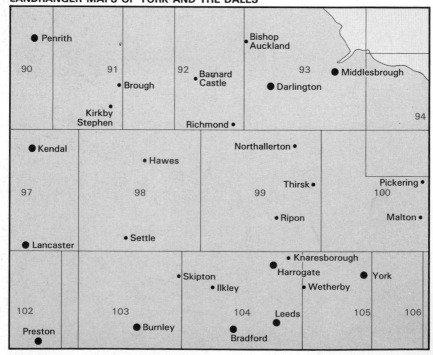

● Penrith

Bishop
Auckland

90   91   92   Barnard   93   ● Middlesbrough
Castle

● Brough   ● Darlington

● Kirkby   94
Stephen   Richmond ●

● Kendal   Northallerton ●

● Hawes   Thirsk ●   Pickering ●

97   98   99   100

● Ripon   Malton ●

● Settle   ● Knaresborough

Harrogate
● Lancaster   ● Skipton   ● York

● Ilkley   ● Wetherby

102   103   104   Leeds   105   106
●

Preston   ● Burnley

●   Bradford

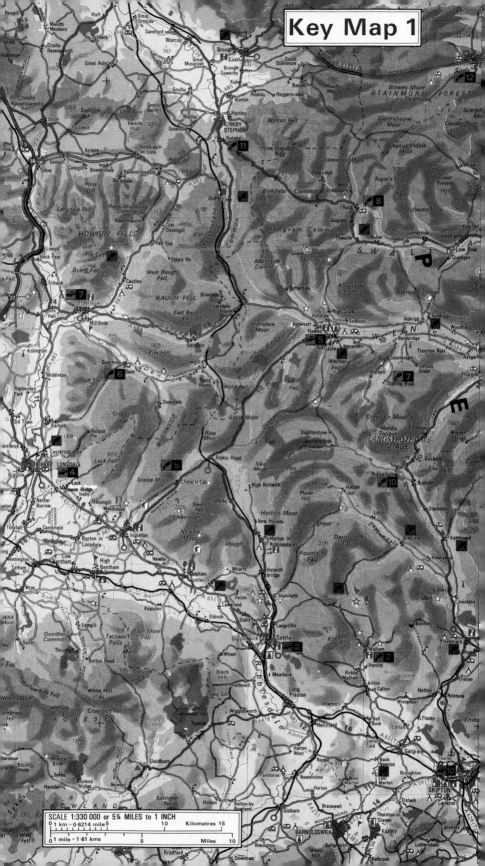

Key Map 1

SCALE 1:330 000 or 5¼ MILES to 1 INCH

0 1 km = 0·6214 mile   5   10   Kilometres 15

0 1 mile = 1·61 kms   5   Miles   10

Key Map 2

SCALE 1:330 000 or 5¼ MILES to 1 INCH

| 0 | 1 km = 0·6214 mile | 5 | | 10 | Kilometres | 15 |

| 0 1 mile = 1·61 kms | | 5 | | Miles | 10 |

Introduction
The Dales

Anyone who has ever visited the Dales comes away with an image of the Dales landscape. A river, often turbulent, threads its way down a narrow, green valley. On either side, the hills rise up, their lower slopes a patchwork of fields laced together by dry stone walls. The walls climb on, away from the fields to rough moorland, often topped by a line of pale, jagged rocks. Down in the valley are the villages and market towns, the stone of the houses echoing the stone of the hilltop high above. It seems a timeless landscape, one that genuinely deserves that well-worn epithet 'unspoiled'. Yet what we see is really quite a modern landscape, and, to understand it, one has to travel back through the long ages of geological time to see how the land was formed, before looking at the far briefer history of human efforts to adapt that landscape to our own ends.

The geology of the Dales is complex, but anyone travelling the whole area soon becomes aware of two very distinctive rocks that break through the surface. The commonest is limestone which gleams palely in the sun from many hilltops, and provides the region with some of its most spectacular features: the great cliffs of Kilnsey Crag and Malham Cove; the gash in the hillside that is Gordale Scar. The other rock is the dark millstone grit, mostly seen in the south and east of the region. It, too, has its own special attractions, weathering into fantastic shapes at Brimham Rocks or standing in massive boulders above Ilkley Moor. They seem very different yet both have a common origin, some 300 million years ago in the Carboniferous Period — a name drawn from the coal formation which marked the period, though little coal is actually

Waterfalls

The falls of the Dales are rightly famous. They occur mainly in the Yoredale rocks, which are sandwiches of limestone, sandstone, and shale. In the Ice Age, blocks of hard stone came loose from their foundations on the weak shale. Once the shale was exposed, it was easily washed away. Then the process started again lower down the valley, resulting in a series of ledges, a staircase down which the hill streams still tumble. Sometimes, the falls appear as sheer drops, Hardraw Force being a classic example. At the top is a lip of hard limestone. Below that is the softer sandstone and, at the very bottom, is the shale, which has been eaten away by the water that now drops well clear to leave a dry path behind the fall. A different pattern appears at the even more famous falls at Aysgarth. Here the glacier that dug out Bishopdale bit deeper into the land than the ice that carved Wensleydale. In falling from the higher level to the lower, the river cut back into the land in a series of ledges, the much-admired falls. Other falls show slightly different characteristics, but all have added a spectacular element to the Dales scenery.

Thornton Force: one of the waterfalls featured on the Falls Walk above Ingleton.

found in the Dales region. Warm, shallow seas washed across the land, and lagoons formed over this area which proved an ideal breeding ground for marine animals that died, decomposed, and left only skeletons and shells which, when compressed, form an important constituent of limestone. The seas advanced or retreated, and mud and sand were washed down on to the limestone to form shale and sandstone. Then, when the seas returned, more limestone was formed.

This process, far more complex than a few sentences can suggest, produced three basic areas. There is one great slab of limestone, known as Great Scar Limestone, that runs from Grassington in the east to Kirkby Lonsdale in the west. You can see the top of this 800-foot deep layer in the famous limestone pavements such as that above Malham Cove. North of that are the Yoredales, like a sandwich cake of mainly limestone and sandstone interspersed with shale. Where the weak shale layers erode, you get caps and shelves of limestone and the typical ledges over which waterfalls cascade. The deeper seas gave us the sandstones that become more dominant in the south. These are the basic building blocks of the scenery. Each stone has its own character which it imparts to a landscape that, in turn, was to undergo yet more traumatic changes. At times, it heaved itself up with volcanic action creating long, deep fissures which were then filled by new material washing in, including valuable minerals. But by far the most important event as far as scenery was concerned was the Ice Age which submerged the whole area beneath snow and ice as recently, geologically speaking, as 20,000 years ago. This was only the last of a series of ice ages. Look up any dale towards its head and it is not difficult to imagine a glacier flowing slowly but inexorably, carving out the valley. The uplands eroded and brought debris down into the valley. Sometimes vast boulders were carried in the glacial flow, only to be left literally high and dry as the ice receded — the Norber boulders of Ingleborough are the best-known example.

So gradually, as the ice retreated, a new landscape appeared. Hills were rounded by the action of ice, though some were left flat-capped as more durable rock survived. The water collects on the uplands: sometimes it cascades down as mountain streams; in other places, it disappears through fissures in the limestone — the pot holes which are also such a feature of the region — to carve out underground caves and follow its own mysterious

Early Humans
The Stone Ages
The record for early Stone Age people is scant in the Dales, but somewhere around 9,000 BC at the end of the Paleolithic Period, the hunter-gatherers appeared, living in caves and venturing out for food. Remains of their habitation have been found at Victoria Cave near Settle. Mesolithic Man has left very few clues to his existence, but the Neolithic or New Stone Age marks a real major turning point in the history of the region. The people of the New Stone Age had a complex civilisation. Their flint tools were remarkably efficient and polished stone axes had cutting edges quite capable of felling trees. From some time around 4,000 BC, they were clearing the woodland, building huts, and establishing farms. They used pottery, and they had a society that could be organised for major works. The outstanding monument of the period in the Dales is Castle Dykes, high on Aysgarth Moor. This is a henge, but with no signs of standing stones, just the bank and ditch. But it remains an impressive work.

The Bronze Age
Bronze was the first metal to be used by people in Britain somewhere around 2,000 BC, but it was many centuries after that before it spread to the hills of the north. By around 1,300 BC, however, stone tools had been replaced by the new metal ones, and there was a period of some wealth when luxury items were produced.

The Iron Age
The use of iron implements, which began about 600 BC, really opened up the area for settlers. These people, collectively known as Celts, represented many different tribes, with the Brigantes predominant. They established ordered settlements. They ploughed the land and one can still see the results of this work in areas such as the moors above Grassington. They also built forts to defend their territory, and the great hilltop plateau of Ingleborough is rimmed with their fortifications. They lived on in the area right through the Roman occupation.

The Romans

Caesar came to Britain In 55-54 BC, but it was the invasion by Claudius in AD 43 that marked the beginning of Roman rule. It also marks the beginning of written history in Britain. The Romans stayed because Britain had commodities that they prized, particularly mineral wealth. The well-armed, well-drilled legions had little difficulty overcoming the resistance of the scattered and disorganised Celtic tribes. Forts were established, joined together by roads constructed with military precision in the straight lines for which Roman roads are famous. The northern half of the country, Britannia Inferior, was governed from the colonia of Eboracum — York, and the city is still rich in Roman remains. The Romans exploited the lead mines of the Dales, but otherwise showed little interest in what they clearly regarded as a hostile environment. They set up forts around the edges to keep control and built their roads across the moors, but once the shock of war had died away, life among the Celtic tribes went on much as before. In AD 306, Constantine the Great was declared Emperor at York, but it was a troubled empire he ruled, attacked from all sides. The British, tired of taxation and increasingly inefficient rule, joined the general rebellion against Rome. In 409, Roman rule was ended.

course until it emerges again into the light. There is an excellent example in miniature in the stream above Chapel-le-Dale, described in **Walk 5**. A rather more spectacular example can be found in Malham. Once, the waters from Malham Tarn would have crashed over the cliffs of the cove in a great waterfall, but now they simply disappear underground and re-emerge at the foot of the cliff. But, by whatever route the waters reach the valley, there they join to form the rivers

Dark Ages

The period between the end of Roman rule and the Norman Conquest was marked by repeated invasions from different quarters: Angles, Saxons, and Norse all came to settle in Britain. These different groups left their mark on the country. Today we mostly know about the Anglo-Saxons through the churches which they founded and the massive, elaborately carved crosses with which they graced them. The Norsemen, the Vikings, had a much more profound effect. The early Viking period of raids and plunder, when the long ships with their fearsomely carved prows travelled up the rivers deep into the heart of the country, gave way to a time of settlement. For a period from 919 to 954, York or Jorvik was capital of a Norse kingdom. The physical remains of the period are scant, but the Norsemen enriched the language and, to this day, the old Dales dialect still has a peppering of Norse words.

which bring fertility to the Dales.

As the ice retreated, so very gradually people advanced, though it was not a very hospitable landscape that greeted them. It was a wilderness of rock and stone carried down by the glaciers which was only slowly being colonised by plants, firstly the tough mosses and grasses, then, as the climate warmed, the trees came — birch first, then pine and hazel. Early humans found refuge in the caves, from which they could go out to fish the lakes and streams or hunt the animals of the forest that was now covering virtually the whole area. As people became more adept at making and using tools of stone and flint, so they were able to venture away from the caves, to clear ground for themselves and to provide pasture for the animals they were now domesticating. The upland clearance allowed water to collect, and gradually nature took over the process people had started. The trees began to lose their hold, and what had been forest became the peat bog which still stains the mountain streams their rich brown colour.

Bit by bit, people mastered new skills. They learned how to smelt ore to make metals, first bronze and then iron. Now they had far better weapons with which to tame the land and the forest gradually retreated before them.

The Iron Age saw the true opening up of the Dales. The axes rang out as they bit into timber and more and more land was cleared for homes. The tribes who settled began making fields — no easy matter in this landscape. The sloping hillsides were easier to clear than the dense forests of the valleys, so they cut back the trees and then created terraces or lynchets on the hillsides. The British tribes, mainly the Brigantes, were confronted by a new civilisation in the first century AD. In AD 71 the Roman legions had occupied the Vale of York and soon conquered the Dales. The Vale was much more to the newcomers' liking than the hill country, and they established a fortress at Eboracum, which was to become the city of York. Having pacified the Dales, they were content to leave a few garrisons to keep things under control, but were then quite happy to allow the local population to get on with its own affairs.

After the Romans left, the British simply continued farming the land, and many of the lynchets from this period are still common features in the landscape. These long strips, divided by their grassy banks, are generally known as Celtic Fields and they can be seen at their best around Grassington and Malham. There was little change to this basic pattern of life in the Dales even when new settlers, such as the Angles, came in. The next wave of immigrant invaders, however, left more permanent records. The Norsemen are generally depicted in popular images as wild men in horned helmets, raiding and plundering the countryside. What they are less often shown as doing is settling on the land for a peaceful life of farming. Yet this is just what they did, and they also took over the old Roman legionary fortress of Eboracum, built new houses of wood, as well as wharfs for their ships which kept them in contact with Scandinavia. They named their new city Jorvik, which in time became York. The story is told in the Jorvik Viking Centre in the city, but traces of the Norse beginnings can be found in the streets. Visitors often wonder

why there are so many street names ending in 'gate', most of which do not lead to gates in the old city wall. The answer is that *gata* is the old Norse name for street. Similarly, the Norsemen gave the Dales many place names. The Viking farmers brought their sheep down to the valley for winter pasture, just as today's farmers do, and, in summer, they established temporary homes, or *saetrs*, in the upland. The name lingers on in hamlets such as Appersett and Countersett. Other villages, such as Wath and Muker, and Arkengarthdale, preserve their Norse names intact. Names of physical features, such as beck, crag, and tarn, come from the Norse — we even owe the name itself, 'dale', to them.

Generations of settlers had established a pattern. They grouped together in villages, many with a central enclosure where stock could be kept at night — areas which now survive as village greens. Around these were the common fields, often clambering up the steeper hillsides in lynchets. Christianity was also taking a hold, and some of the massive crosses from the period survive, the most impressive being outside Masham church. This basic pattern was to survive for many centuries, but the Norman Conquest brought its own pattern of life, superimposed on the old. Two new powers appeared in the land, and both have left behind magnificent memorials. The Norman lords built themselves strongholds, and it is easy to see how the important towns of the region, such as Richmond and Skipton, grew up under the protection of the castle. York was already an

The tall keep of Richmond Castle rising high above the River Swale.

impressive provincial city, and it continued to grow under Norman patronage. The old population was less than enthusiastically welcoming; the spasmodic rebellions were put down with great ruthlessness and the land parcelled out among the new Norman landlords. The old forests were declared to be their privileged hunting grounds and many areas which had once been farmed were left desolate and empty by this 'harrowing of the North' of 1069.

The other growing power in the land was the Church, to which the beauty and magnificence of York Minster offers eloquent testimony. For some, the growing wealth of York sat uneasily with vows of poverty and austerity, and monks left to found their own monasteries which they intended to keep close to the original ideals. Fountains Abbey meant to be just such a place, but ironically grew to become one of the most powerful and wealthiest institutions in the area. They owned vast tracts of land: the name Fountains Fell for the area of open land to the north of Settle is no mere coincidence, for this was indeed part of the Abbey's estates. A waggon road can still be traced, sometimes as a modern road and sometimes as a broad green lane, stretching all the way from the Fell back to the Abbey. One of the more interesting sections is Mastiles Lane which runs from just south of Malham Tarn across the moor to Kilnsey. Here was the Abbey Grange, the administrative centre for the area — sadly, however, little remains but a few fragments incorporated into farm buildings. And over this whole tract great flocks of sheep roamed free, for ultimately the wealth of the abbeys rested on wool. Between them, the great abbeys and priories controlled most of the land in the Dales.

The most significant event in determining the pattern of Dales life was the Dissolution of the monasteries by Henry VIII. The living quarters of the great houses were destroyed, the roofs of their churches removed. Stones were taken away by locals as useful building materials, and all that remained were the walls and carved pillars of the churches and the elegant stone tracery of windows through which the winds now blew free. These are the ruins which attract visitors today and, while it is easy to see the beauty of Fountains, Bolton, or Jervaulx, it is not always so easy to glimpse the power they once represented, a power which came to such an abrupt end. The old estates were sold off to wealthy merchants and to the gentry, who then sold them on again to the tenant farmers. At that time, the Dales scenery was very different from that which we know today. The monastic estates had been largely unfenced and unwalled, open moorland over which the sheep wandered at will. The farmhouses were poor affairs of timber. But the new generation of freeholders now had an incentive to improve both farm and land. In the seventeenth century, the modern Dales landscape we so much admire today began to appear.

The old farmhouses had been based on the 'cruck'. Two curved timbers meet to form an arch, which could be joined to a

Bolton Priory in its romantic setting beside the River Wharfe.

Railways in The Dales

The Dales present an obviously difficult terrain for railway construction, and were never very well served; of the lines that were built most have now closed. For once, the blame cannot be laid at the door of Dr Beeching — the lines did not survive long enough to feel his axe. But what a delight they must have been: to the north, a line reached across from Barnard Castle and Kirkby Stephen; in the heart of the area was what would have been a wonderfully scenic line from Northallerton, passing through such spots as Jervaulx, Wensley, Aysgarth, and Hawes to Garsdale — part of this route is still used for freight. One of the most spectacular, and shortest lived, was the light railway that ran up Nidderdale all the way to Scar House Reservoir. To the west, a line ran from Clapham, through Ingleton to Sedbergh and Low Gill. In the south, a line snaked up from Skipton to Grassington, but some at least of the lines in this part still carry trains — and there are plans for more track to be brought into use. The following are the principal railways still in use.

The Settle and Carlisle

So far as scenery is concerned, this has the reputation of being the finest railway in all England. It connects with the main route from Skipton and, for the present at least, still carries passenger trains. It is also a popular route for steam excursions, and there are few grander sights on the railways than that of a main-line express

The Yorkshire Dales Railway at Embsay.

hauling a full train up the grades or steaming across Ribblehead viaduct.

The Yorkshire Dales Railway

This preserved steam railway runs from the delightful little station at Embsay, which celebrated its centenary in 1988. There are plans to extend the line back along its old route to Bolton Abbey.

The Keighley and Worth Valley Railway

This steam railway is unusual in that the whole of the branch line from Keighley to Oxenhope has been preserved. The stations, which include Haworth, have all been beautifully restored. The line became well known as the setting for the film, The Railway Children.

Leyburn to Redmire

Occasional passenger excursions are organised on this freight line, but the route is also followed by the Dales Rail service, which uses buses to connect with the Settle and Carlisle line at Garsdale.

second arch by purlins and strengthened by the beams. Strength depended on the height and width of the cruck, and there was a limit to the length of timber available. So a building would consist of a series of boxes or bays — some used for living quarters, some as barns — each box more or less 12 feet long and 16 feet wide, the sides formed of wattle and daub. The new freehold farmers replaced the old farm buildings by new ones in stone, but saw no reason to change the pattern of the building. Houses were still divided into bays, with barns and living quarters under a roof of stone flags. But, just as the size of timber determined the size of the timber house, so the stone available had its effect on building. Large blocks of

stone were scarce, so openings were kept small. The result is a long, low stone house with mullioned windows and a door which often has a seventeenth-century date carved above it. One of the finest examples is West New House in Bishopdale, built in 1635.

The new generation of farmers also had to mark out their land to distinguish it from the neighbours'. They now needed their own fields to grow hay which could then be stored in a barn as winter feed for sheep and cattle. So they built stone walls, walls that marched up the fells and divided the valleys into neat squares and rectangles, and in these valley fields they built simple stone barns. What we think of as the traditional farming landscape of

Lead Mining

The Romans mined lead in the Dales, and the great abbeys controlled extensive mineral rights, but the visible evidence of mining which we can see today seldom dates back beyond the seventeenth century.

Lead ore, galena, generally exists as narrow veins that go down deep into the earth. The first essential stage is finding the veins. Traditionally, this was done by 'hushing'. Streams were temporarily dammed, then allowed to flood out, washing away the surface soil to reveal the mineral. The earliest type of mine working which has left a clear mark in the landscape is the 'bell pit'. Here, a shallow shaft is sunk down, then the miners work out from the base to leave a bell-shaped cavity. The spoil thrown up to the surface leaves a characteristic ring around the shaft, and there are many examples on the moors above Grassington. Eighteenth-century technology allowed deeper pits to be sunk, and tunnels were dug into the veins from the hillside.

The ore that came to the surface had to be separated from the other rock and then cleaned. This involved washing the ore and, in the more sophisticated processes, 'buddles' were used. These circular stone saucers were washed with water, which allowed the heavy lead ore to settle in the centre and the lighter waste material was left at the edge — like an overgrown version of the gold miner's pan. To get the pure metal, the ore needed to be smelted, heated in a furnace that would burn off unwanted elements such as sulphur. Unfortunately, the lead could vaporise in the process and be lost with the smoke up the chimney. The solution to that problem produced one of the characteristic features of Dales lead mining, the moorland flue and its chimney. The flue was, in effect, a very long chimney which, instead of sticking up in the air, was laid down on the slope of a hill. In this the gases from the furnace cooled and the lead condensed, or sublimated, before it reached the conventional chimney high on the moor. There are good examples of smelt mines in the area, particularly in Swaledale. A century ago, the low price of imported lead led to closure of the last of the mines.

This little stone building in Arkengarthdale was used to house gunpowder for blasting in the nearby lead mines.

Locks on the Leeds and Liverpool Canal at Bank Newton.

the Dales had finally arrived.

The eighteenth century brought its own changes. Improved quarrying techniques and better transport provided for a new generation of grander and often more comfortable houses. There was a busy passage of pack animals over the moors, and the many pack-horse bridges are reminders of those times. The animals, moving in single file, each carrying panniers strapped to their flanks, could easily cope with high arches and narrow roadways, but parapets were kept low so that the panniers could swing clear of them. The new turnpike roads, which were paid for by fees charged to travellers, began to open up the area to new influences. Even that most important transport route of the age, the canal, put in an appearance, as the Leeds and Liverpool Canal skirted the southern edge of the Dales. All around the edges the effects of the Industrial Revolution were felt, and wool, linen, and cotton mills appeared. They even reached as high in the Dales as Aysgarth and Hawes. But for most of the people hand crafts were far more important. Spinning the wool and knitting, mostly for hosiery, were vital to the Dales economy. The mineral wealth of the area took on a new importance. Lead had been mined in Roman times, and lead from the Dales was sent to line the roof of York Minster, but now mining and smelting the ore became an important industry and has left its own characteristic marks on the landscape — sometimes just a muddle of

humps and hollows on the ground, in other places a lonely moorland hill can be seen to be topped by the tall chimney of a smelter.

The nineteenth century gave a new phenomenon to the region — the railway. York was the capital for a railway empire that extended from Rugby in the Midlands to Newcastle in the north, and the undisputed king of this new realm was George Hudson. He pulled together small companies to make a great railway, the Midland. He also promoted a vast number of new lines which showed often quite illusory paper profits. When the extent of his double dealing was exposed, Hudson the Railway King fell as rapidly and completely as he had risen. Yet he did leave behind a genuine legacy of real achievements, which is why York was an appropriate place in which to establish a great National Railway Museum. The Dales, however, were never very promising terrain for railway construction. The principal route in the area was a reflection of the piecemeal nature of Victorian railway development. The profit of individual companies was more important than any overall sensible pattern of transport. So when the Midland Railway wanted access to Scotland and applied to use the existing eastern route over Shap Fell, the London North Western would have none of it. So the Midland had to build their own line from Settle to Carlisle over some hopelessly inappropriate countryside. Railway enthusiasts still love the line, but there is no denying that in any rational transport system it would never have been built. Other routes penetrated the region

— down Wensleydale and Wharfedale and up the valley of the Nidd. They carried goods and local people — and they also brought a new industry to the region, tourism.

Scenery was virtually invented at the end of the eighteenth century. Before that time, travellers cautiously skirted round the outside of the Dales. Daniel Defoe, who visited the area in the 1720s, dismissed the fells as 'barren and frightful', and decided that no more need be said on the subject as '...'tis of no advantage to represent horror'. But, by the end of the century, picturesque scenery became a vogue, and travellers rushed off to admire the hills and mountains of Derbyshire and the Lake District. A few visited the Dales.

One visitor discovered Gordale Scar which certainly impressed him, if the flurry of capital letters and exclamation marks are any guide:

'Good Heavens! What was my Astonishment! — The Alps, the Pyrenées, Loch Lomond, or any other Wonder of the Kind at no time exhibit such a Chasm.'

Artists began to take an interest in the area, notably J M W Turner who produced an immense number of works covering all aspects from the peaceful lake of Semer Water to the grandeur of the Malham scenery. The idea of a wild, romantic countryside in Yorkshire was given added impetus by the work of the Brontë sisters. For many the image of a Yorkshire moor will always be associated

The Brontës

There is no more extraordinary family in English literature than the Brontës. Here are three sisters brought up in a remote Yorkshire village, in a family which, if not actually poor, was certainly far from wealthy, who produced a series of accepted masterpieces. And none of them lived to celebrate their fortieth birthdays. Over a century after their deaths, their works are still read, and still help to shape the mental image that we have of the Yorkshire countryside.

Their father's achievements are seldom mentioned, but are, in their way, almost as impressive as those of his daughters. He was born Patrick Brunty, the eldest of ten children of a farmer in County Down. He taught

Haworth church.

himself to read and write and was appointed to teach in a village school. There the local vicar encouraged him to go on with his education and he eventually gained a Cambridge degree and entered the church, having also changed his name to Brontë. He took his first curacy in 1806 and, in 1812, he married Maria Branwell. There were six children — Maria, Elizabeth, Charlotte, Patrick Branwell, Emily, and Anne.

In 1820, the family moved to the home which will always be associated with the Brontës, the Parsonage in Haworth, set on the edge of the moor in a countryside that was almost to seem like a living character in the sisters' works. It was not a happy move for Maria Brontë who died the following year, and her sister 'Aunt Branwell' moved in to look after the children and stayed in Haworth for twenty years. It was during this period that the girls first began to show their talents, with vivid stories written for their own amusement. That happy time came to an end in 1824 when the girls, except for Anne, were sent off to Cowan Bridge near Kirkby Lonsdale to a school for clergymen's daughters. The discipline was harsh and the conditions atrocious, and it was to have a devastating effect on the family. Maria and Elizabeth both died, and the other girls were hastily brought home. The experience found its way into Jane Eyre.

The three surviving girls continued steadily with their education, but Branwell's life tottered from disaster to disaster. He failed at every job he tried, became an all-too-regular visitor at the Black Bull in Haworth and then took to

with the passionate lovers of *Wuthering Heights*. The walkers and the sightseers who arrived in the area by rail came at just the right time, for traditional industries, such as lead mining, were in serious decline by the end of the nineteenth century and were soon to disappear altogether.

Tourism has reached new peaks in the twentieth century, and has brought both prosperity and problems to the area. The visitors come to see the traditional landscape of old market towns and villages, the open fells, and the romantic windswept moors. But they bring with them cars that need parking and caravans that need a place to rest. Narrow roads that have served a quiet agricultural community for centuries seem less appropriate to the motor car age. The 'unspoiled' villages are often largely occupied by holiday-makers and weekenders, and even the pattern of farming is changing. It is temptingly easy for a hard-pressed hill farmer to abandon the old, slow skills of dry stone walling for manufactured fence posts and wire. Even the walkers create problems of erosion as thousands of heavy-booted feet tramp over such popular routes as the Pennine Way and the Dales Way.

In spite of all the problems, the Dales retain their magic. It is still possible to drive on roads where traffic jams mean waiting behind a flock of sheep or a herd of cows ambling down to the milking

The Brontë memorial chapel in Haworth church, completed in 1964.

opium. He died of tuberculosis at the age of thirty-one. The girls, meanwhile, all set off into new careers as governesses — and all hated it. Emily, in particular, was desperately homesick for Haworth and its moors, and her love of that landscape illuminates the whole of her great work, Wuthering Heights. Anne, too, pined for Haworth though she also found a new love in the Yorkshire coast. Charlotte's work had taken her to the heart of the textile district, to an area dominated by the woollen mills of Halifax and Dewsbury. Her early years had introduced her to the older world of handloom weavers of Haworth and the surrounding villages. She used the conflict of these two worlds for her novel, Shirley. But, though the girls made full use of what came their way as governesses, they were sufficiently unhappy to decide to give up that life. They came together again at Haworth, determined to start a school of their own.

Charlotte, accompanied for a time by Emily, went to Brussels to gain wider experience of teaching. There she fell in love — and the love was not returned. Sad and miserable she returned to Haworth, but, in true Brontë fashion, she was to transmute the experience into literature, in two of her lesser-known novels, Villette and The Professor.

The school never materialised, but the sisters took up writing in earnest under pseudonyms based on their initials — Currer, Acton, and Ellis Bell. In an extraordinary period between 1846 and 1849 the family knew success and tragedy. Charlotte's Jane Eyre, Emily's Wuthering Heights, and Anne's Agnes Grey were all published in 1847. But, by 1849, Emily aged twenty-nine and Anne aged thirty-one were dead, killed like Branwell by consumption. Now Charlotte was left alone to care for her ageing father.

She continued to write and, although she was shy by nature, the secret of her identity was bound to be revealed eventually. She began to travel and was widely fêted as one of the principal literary figures of the age. But, when at last she came to marry, her husband was not of that world. She married her father's curate, Arthur Nicholls. It was a short-lived marriage: the wedding was held in June 1854. In March the following year Charlotte, the last of the sisters, was buried in Haworth churchyard.

Lady Anne Clifford

This remarkable lady was born at Skipton Castle in 1590, the daughter of George, Earl of Cumberland. Her father soon left the north of England — but his daughter never lost her love of it. When the earl died, he left his Yorkshire estates to his brother and began a legal battle that was to last nearly forty years. A deed of Edward II entailed the estate on the child, male or female, and Anne was the only surviving child. She fought for her rights with persistence and courage, taking her case right up to the king himself. But it was only when the brother died, to be followed shortly afterwards by his only son, that Anne Clifford came into her own. She was now nearly sixty, but was to spend the next quarter-century putting her estates in order.

She began with Skipton Castle, which had been largely pulled down in the Civil War, and at once started rebuilding giving the castle the appearance it has today. She then set out to do the same to her other castles — Appleby, Brougham, Brough, and Pendragon — and she restored Barden Tower. Not content with that, she set to work arranging for the restoration of churches, chapels, and almshouses on her estates. To the very end of her life, she travelled her beloved Dales, viewing with great satisfaction the works she had set in hand. She died in 1676 and was buried in Appleby church.

Barden Tower.

sheds. There are villages which are still made up of old stone houses and a village green with a friendly pub at the side and the tower of an ancient church showing above the trees. And it is still possible to walk lonely paths where the only companions are the piping curlews and the rabbits scampering for safety. Can it survive? It can do, but only if an effort is made to ensure that it survives. The National Park Authority is the most important conservation body in the area but, in the long term, the future of the Dales will depend on the people who live there and those who visit. If the locals are given help and encouragement, then one can be sure that they will be as keen as anyone to preserve this unique landscape. But it is equally important that those who come to the Dales show respect. They must also perhaps be prepared to put up with some inconvenience. It may be an irritation to have to reverse back to a stopping place on a single-track road, but that road may be one of the elements that contribute to the charm of the region. Widen it, improve it — and some essential part of the character of the place may be lost forever. Not so long ago, cars could drive right up to Brimham Rocks, so that there was more painted metal than sandstone to look at. The new separate car park has brought the Rocks back to their old magnificence. Few now regret the change. A similar thoughtful approach taken elsewhere will ensure that this unique and supremely beautiful region of Britain never loses its appeal.

The Natural History of The Dales

It is almost a misnomer to speak of the 'natural' history of the Dales for, when we look out on moorland and valley farm, we are looking at an environment largely created by people. There is scarcely a part of the whole region which would look as it does now if people were simply to leave it alone — or perhaps it would be more accurate to say if their stock left it alone.

Within the Dales, sheep farming predominates, and three types of land usually occur within the area used by any individual farmer. The traditional farm has a small area in the valley floor, given over to hay meadows which can also be rich with wild flowers. Modern intensive farming methods, however, have tended to produce fields with higher grass yields which, sadly, can only be achieved at the expense of the flowers. But whether traditional farm or modern, the valleys are a brilliant green, watered by the rivers and the many becks draining down off the surrounding fells. Traditionally, the sheep graze the meadows in spring before being turned off to allow the hay to grow. That was harvested and stored in the field barns which could also house the cattle in the winter. So the overall appearance of the valley floor very much depends on the cycle of the farming year. The poor quality of the soil ensures that crops other than hay are virtually unknown in the region.

The next section of farmland is the rough pasture that spreads up the lower slopes away from the valley floor. This is where the sheep and cattle graze during the haymaking season. Above and beyond that are the moors and fells, where the grazing is scant, but where the heather moors form an ideal breeding ground for grouse. One obvious result of having so many busily munching sheep is that young shoots rarely have a chance to develop. As mentioned in the previous chapter, this area was once heavily forested but, once it was cleared, the trees never had a chance to recolonise. One can get some idea of what would happen without the flocks by looking at areas of land which they cannot reach. The disused railway described in **Walk 11** has deep cuttings protected by fences and is already showing a good stock of flourishing saplings. There are woodland areas but, increasingly, the tree cover that is seen in the Dales consists of the solid green masses of new conifer plantations. These are spreading throughout the British countryside, largely due to the tax advantages given to those who pay for them. The plantations are seldom owned by local people, but are simply an investment guaranteed a good return. The dense forests offer no scope for any other form of life to thrive, and their effect on the qualities and beauty of the landscape is invariably disastrous. It could be argued that it is people and their farming that give the area its present character, so why should the forests be any different? The answer is simple: the old methods allowed for a rich variety of plant and animal life to thrive; the conifer plantations simply monopolise the land on which they stand.

The natural history of the region has, then, been shaped by people, but people's activity is no more than one factor that determines what will grow and flourish where. And, just as the pattern of human settlement has depended on the age-old forces of climate and weather, so too does the pattern of plant development. And on that also depends the animal life of the region.

The Uplands

The upland areas can conveniently be divided into two groups: the grasslands associated with the limestone, and the moorland that belongs with the millstone grit and the shales. The limestone region that stretches across the southern dales is notable for the springy turf that makes walking in the area such a delight. There are excellent examples of this type of landscape in two of the walks described later — the walk above Malham and that above Hubberholme. Walkers should give thanks to the sheep, those efficient, tireless lawn mowers of the region. The commonest grass is sheep's fescue which, as the name suggests, makes particularly nutritious feeding. Flowers also flourish in the area, particularly the delicate hare-

Grazing sheep have had a profound influence on the Dales landscape.

Two plants to be found on the limestone hills above Malham: wild thyme (left); and the common rock rose (right).

bell and purple wild thyme. Other flowers are perhaps less obvious but thrive in the limestone region — yellow rock rose, salad burnet, and eyebright.

Both of these grassy walks also show another typical feature of the area, the limestone pavement. The grikes, the deep clefts that break up the pavement, are moist and shady and rich in lime. For plant life conditions are not unlike those of a woodland floor, and similar plants can be found — hart's-tongue fern and spleenworts, wood anemone, and wild garlic are all to be seen. Secure in their clefts, they are as well protected from the nibbling sheep as they are from the elements. More surprisingly, trees can also thrive on the pavements. Usually the occasional solitary hawthorn, bent and stunted by the high winds, is all that is to be seen. Yet other trees can and do thrive, notably ash. There is a splendid example on the scar at the north end of Ingleborough. Colt Park Wood can be seen running parallel to the B6479. Here the ash stand directly on the clints, the limestone blocks, their roots reaching down into the grikes, and they are also joined by other trees, including rowan and cherry. One of the most important plants of the limestone is the one most easily overlooked. Look out across at the stone and it seems pallid, almost white, though the stone itself is a dull grey. The brightness comes from the lichens that cover the rock and also, slowly and gradually, eat it away, giving the pavements the characteristic rounded edges.

The moors that overlie the shales and gritstones have very different appearances. The highest moors are covered in peat and, if walking on the limestone grasslands can seem to be just about ideal, the same could not be said of these areas of squelchy bog and rough tussocks. The rocks create the difference.

The fissured limestone allows surface water to drain away with great speed; the impermeable sandstone holds it. The overall effect is not improved by the fact that many of the plants, such as the mosses, are also good at retaining water. The typical plant of the peat moor is cotton grass which, in early summer, produces the white heads like cotton balls which give it its name. Bog moss or sphagnum is also common and thrives on the mires that are filled-in tarns. Walking across these is an uncomfortable experience, like tramping across a giant jelly. Wiry bilberry and crowberry can be seen, and the plant which, more than any other, adds brilliance and colour to the

The dark rock of one of the Norber boulders, carried here by glaciers, contrasts with the limestone.

The Yorkshire Dales National Park

The National Park is one of ten set up in the 1950s to help preserve some of the finest landscape in the country. In the Dales there are very clear objectives: first and foremost to protect the scenery with its wild plants and animals. They are also concerned to preserve the essential character of the artificial environment — the stone villages, the barns and stone walls — and to keep the essential rural nature of the area intact. The Park Authority does not itself own the land, so one of its prime aims is to ensure that it has a good working relationship with those who do. As the Authority is always keen to point out, it does not wish to turn the Dales into an oversized theme Park, a kind of giant rural museum. People live and work in the region, and it would be a sorry day for the Dales if it ever became a fossilised landscape full of holiday homes. There is, however, also a realisation that tourism is here to stay, and the National Park authorities are there to ensure that those who visit the Dales find it a rewarding experience. Apart from the necessary administrators there are seven main groups at work.

Landscape Conservation

The section deals with landowners, persuading them to retain such important features as hay meadows and broadleaved woodland. An important aspect is the free advisory service on how to combine conservation with profitable farming.

Development Control

This deals with planning applications. Change and development are essential to any community, but the National Park authorities have to make sure that new development does not destroy the character of the Dales.

Built Environment

This is the positive side of conservation: working to preserve and restore historic buildings and villages.

Warden Service

The National Park wardens are the people on the spot, each of the six responsible for one area of the park, with the help of assistants and volunteers.

Access and Recreation

The main part of the section's work is ensuring that rights of way are kept open.

Three Peaks Project

The Three Peaks are popular with walkers — almost too popular — and the project has been set up to repair the damage done by the many booted feet that have trooped these hills.

Information Services

These are just what the name suggests. They run the six National Park centres.

Whernside Centre

This is the Park's own outdoor study and recreation centre, which runs a wide range of courses. It is not always easy to see what the National Park team have done, but look round some other rural areas, and it is all too easy to see what might have happened to the Dales without them.

moorland scene — heather. This flourishes on dry ground, which can come with natural drought or through human intervention. It can be seen in the old lead mining areas where the land is drained, but it is commonest on the managed moors where it is especially coveted. For the heather is the natural habitat of the red grouse, which feed on the young shoots. The vast expanses of purple that add so much beauty to the moorland scene are there, in some measure at least, because gentlemen wish to shoot birds. The grouse are not, however, the only local inhabitants that enjoy a delicate young heather shoot. Sheep also enjoy it, so gamekeepers and farmers have a common interest in controlling the heather moor, by burning off the old heather while ensuring that invaders such as mat grass do not take over. Bracken also flourishes in this moorland environment, but can be easily controlled by allowing cattle to graze on the slopes. Once again, it is human intervention that has produced what might seem to be a wholly natural, untouched environment. Down on the moor's edge, a variety of different plants grow, the familiar white mat grass gives a pallid border but, in damper areas, the blue moor-grass takes over. Touches of colour come with spearworts and eyebright.

Woodland

The other great difference between the millstone grit area and the limestone region is the presence of a far greater woodland cover than that of the scar woods. Yet what we see today has been much affected by people. The Normans planted oak in the deer forests which once covered a large part of the area. The next important planting period was the eighteenth century. The taste for parkland developed by the great landscape gardeners, such as Capability Brown, spread throughout the country. Landowners planted trees simply to improve the appearance of the scenery — and it says something of their confidence that they did so knowing that the effect would hardly be appreciated within their own lifetimes. There are many examples in the Dales, the extensive park that spreads west from Wensley being a fine one. This area also shows examples of two other varieties of plantation — those which provide cover for game birds and those which supply shelter for farm animals. But, for most people, it is not the obviously artificial parklands that attract attention, but the remnants of the older woods and forests.

The most famous and certainly the most popular wooded area in the Dales is in Wharfedale, stretching upstream from Bolton Abbey, beyond the Strid to Barden Bridge. Here the dominant tree is the sessile oak. It is not easily distinguished from the common oak, the principal features of note being stalkless acorns and longer-stalked leaves. The overall shape of the sessile oak tends to be slightly different, the straight, spreading branches giving a shapelier, more open crown. This wood also has a number of exotic species, specially planted here. The Strid Woods are the best known, but they are by no means the only large areas of oak woodland, though they all tend to be found on the eastern edge of the Dales in Wensleydale and Nidderdale as well as Wharfedale. But, wherever they occur, they have great visual appeal. In autumn the woods have a golden radiance while, in spring, the more delicate shades of other trees in the wood, especially birch and larch, predominate. Alder, ash, sycamore, and willow are all to be found in the woods alongside the oak.

The oak woods of the valleys have a floor rich in nutrients, so that there is an accompanying richness to the ground cover. There is an undergrowth of brambles, hawthorn, hazel, and holly, but the real attraction is the carpet of flowers. The predominant colours are whites and yellows — lesser celandine, wood anemone, wood sorrel, and wild garlic, but, in

Woodland plants. The lesser celandine (top) flowers in the spring and prefers damp woodland. Wood sorrel (bottom), another spring bloomer, is a creeping plant that closes its leaves at night.

late spring, the woodland floor seems to be covered in a pale blue haze as the bluebells come into flower.

Although it is by no means as common as in other parts of the country, the area does contain woodland planted for timber — not the blanketing conifers of the modern age, but a mixture of broadleaved trees and conifers. Mostly these were planted in the nineteenth century. One area of woodland that is still managed along traditional lines is Freeholders' Wood by Aysgarth Falls, now in the care of the National Park. The hazels are coppiced. The timber is cut right back to the wide bole of the tree, which promptly begins sending up new shoots. These grow at a quite remarkable rate, as much as 3 feet a year, and, after about seven years, they can be cut and the whole cycle starts again.

On higher ground the woodland is more sparse. The soil is thinner and nutrients tend to leach away down the slope. The oak still predominates, but the other common species are birch, mountain ash and, on occasions, pine. The woodland floor no longer supports the same rich variety of plant life, and the undergrowth tends to be limited to the typical bracken and tufted, waving grasses of the moorland. The Dales offer one other special type of woodland, that of the gills. Some of the finest of these gill woods are the least accessible. Long Gill, for example, is familiar to walkers on the Pennine Way, but to few others. It lies 3 miles north of Horton-in-Ribblesdale, at the end of a minor road that continues as a track through High Birkwith. The ravine carves a way through wild limestone country between the 300- and 400-metre contours. The Cam Beck charges down the gorge in a series of waterfalls and cascades between high, steep hillsides. It is very difficult for people to investigate on foot — and is especially inhospitable to sheep, which of course accounts for the trees. Ash and hazel line the banks, and, beneath their shade, sheltered from the elements, a luxuriant carpet of flowers and ferns can grow. There are examples to be found throughout the region, though few quite as spectacular as this. Some gills have different dominant species. The deep gill above Askrigg, through which the Whitfield Gill Force tumbles, for example, is notable for its fine beech trees. But whatever the trees that make their home in the deep gills, they are always memorable features, dark green, shady clefts that bring a special richness to moorland and fell.

The Valleys

The valley floors have far richer soils than the uplands, and the result is the typical luxurious hay meadow. Visitors from outside the region sometimes just see these as 'green fields', and think no more about them. They are, in fact, crop fields just as much as a field of wheat or barley, and anyone walking in the area should remember that, when footpaths cross them, the notices asking walkers to move in single file should be obeyed. In most parts of Britain, the natural hay meadow is a rarity, but mercifully survives in the Dales. Instead of the uniformity of the modern farm of other areas, here there is a rich diversity of grasses and, more importantly, an equally rich mixture of flowering herbs. Swaledale is particularly noted for its meadows, and anyone visiting the area in June will not see green fields, but yellow — not the violent yellow of the all-too-familiar rape fields, but a rich, varied hue that comes with fields of buttercups, globe flower, meadow vetchling, and birdsfoot trefoil. As the summer

The meadows of Swaledale are noted for their summer flowers. The globe flower (left) *is a brilliant yellow, but the bird's-foot trefoil* (right) *has a more orange tint.*

Red clover colours the late summer meadows.

advances, the meadows become paler with pignut and sweet cicely adding a rich creamy white to the scene. The brighter colours are supplied by the brilliant purple splashes of wood cranesbill and by red clover.

In traditional Dales farming, the herbs are allowed to seed before the hay is cut, thus ensuring that the brilliance and splendour of the meadows will continue on from year to year. There are few more glorious sights in June than the hay meadows in flower, and their unique qualities have been officially recognised. In 1987, the Ministry of Agriculture designated parts of the Dales as Environmentally Sensitive Areas. It recognised that farmers need to make a living and that modern techniques can improve productivity — but only at the expense of an ecologically impoverished landscape. So a scheme was set up whereby farmers received extra payments for keeping within Ministry guidelines. This involves agreeing not to plough up and reseed meadows, limiting the use of fertilisers and herbicides which favour grasses at the expense of the wild flowers, and not draining the land, so that wetland species can be preserved. Within a year, farmers owning almost two-thirds of the land in the designated area had joined the scheme. A similar scheme was also set up by the National Park authority. If the character of the Dales is to survive, then it is vital that such a scheme should succeed.

Lakes and Rivers

The rivers are the ever-present features of the Dales, constantly fed by water draining down from the hills. In such an area, they undergo quite violent changes in mood and character. It is possible to walk beside a river on two consecutive days and not recognise it as the same watercourse. An example which will be familiar to every visitor to the region is the little

The beautiful River Greta flowing through the woodland at Brignall Banks.

Both the golden eagle (left) *and the smaller merlin* (right) *are occasional visitors to Upper Nidderdale.*

waterfall by the bridge in the centre of Hawes. In dry weather it is a pleasant sight, with clear water splashing down in a series of miniature waterfalls. But, after heavy rain, the waters are swelled by a network of rivulets that join forces all the way from the top of Dodd Fell, 4 miles to the south of the village with a summit over 1300 feet above it. The moorland water drains down off the peat and swells the beck, and the little waterfall becomes a single creamy brown torrent that thunders under the bridge and roars on down to the Ure.

Some of the rivers of this region are noted for their fish — trout in the Wharfe, and, to the west, salmon in the Lune. Elsewhere the commonest fish are roach, grayling, barbel, and dace.

Natural lakes are not a major feature of this region, and there are only two of any size: Malham Tarn and Semer Water. The tarn is somewhat unusual in being at such a high altitude, at approximately 1300 feet above sea level, in the middle of limestone. It is fed by spring water and surrounded by an interesting wetland environment. At the southern end, there are areas of sedge and moss, while at the higher northern end, moorland plants eventually give way to scrubby woodland. At Tarn House visitors can get permits to use a wetland trail laid out as a broadwalk. Most of the floor of the tarn is covered in algae, but it supports a healthy insect population, and perch and trout have been introduced. Semer Water is basically very similar, but here the waters are particularly rich in plankton. This provides good feeding for bream, crayfish, and perch.

These natural lakes cover a far smaller area than the artificial lakes, the reservoirs that are now such an important feature in some parts. The most significant is the string of reservoirs in the Washburn Valley and Nidderdale. They have become very significant and have had a very dramatic impact as far as one aspect of the natural history is concerned — its bird life.

The curlew's (top) *distinctive, ringing cry; the oystercatcher's* (centre) *far shriller call; and the redshank's* (bottom) *yelping cry are all to be heard on the moorland.*

Birds

Having just mentioned the reservoirs, they are an obvious place to start this survey, though the bird life is scarcely typical of

Birds of river and stream.

heron

dipper

kingfisher

sand martin

sandpiper

the Dales as a whole. Yorkshire Water issues special birdwatching permits for many of the reservoirs, and the ornithologist may well be rewarded with sightings of some splendid visitors. All the reservoirs function as winter resorts for wildfowl. Gouthwaite Reservoir is particularly fine and is now a nature reserve — and it is not difficult to see why. In a period from 1950 to 1975, over 200 species of birds were recorded. Of these, the most exciting regular visitor is the osprey, which pauses on its travels and can occasionally be seen fishing here. Scar House Reservoir at the very top of Nidderdale has a very different character. Set high up in the moorland, it has become noted for its birds of prey, and, in recent years, golden eagles have been regularly sighted.

The presence of birds of prey at Scar House is particularly welcome as they have been almost totally removed from the area by gamekeepers protecting the grouse moors. The grouse themselves are an inescapable presence in the heather moors and, even when they are not seen in brief whirring flight, they are seldom out of earshot. The other large bird which can be seen on the moors is the short-eared owl which, unlike the tawny owl, can be seen during daylight hours gliding noiselessly across the landscape. The merlin is also making something of a comeback on the moorland.

The other moorland inhabitants which are as likely to be heard as seen are the waders. The curlew's somewhat mournful cry occasionally gives way to more cheerful song. They winter on the coast but come back to the moors in the spring as a most welcome visitor, and are easily recognised by their long, downward-curved bills. To the plaintive cry of the curlew is added the shrill, staccato 'pick, pick' of the handsome oystercatcher and the more attractive cries of golden plovers, redshanks, and lapwings, the latter known locally as tewits. But of all the bird calls to be heard in the open moorland, none can match the melodic song of the skylark. In spring and early summer, the male rises to hover almost motionless to deliver his aria before drifting slowly back down to the ground. At the opposite end of the musical scale is the little dunlin whose most characteristic calls are a sort of hoarse grunting, though the male claiming his territory is more tuneful.

The meadows of the valleys, with their plentiful flowers, attract a large insect population, which in turn provides good feeding for the birds. The meadow pipit is common in the fields, and swallows and house martins can be seen swooping and diving over the meadows. Both pied and yellow wagtails are often seen.

The woodlands are a favourlte habitat for many birds: woodpeckers, blue tits, nuthatches, and dunnocks, but the most commonly seen is the species introduced by the landowners, the pheasant. It is ironic that of all the birds likely to be met out on a day's walk in the woods, the pheasant is least likely to show concern at your presence — yet its fate is to be shot — while other more nervous birds will survive unscathed.

The rivers and becks also have their own populations. Herons play at statues at the water's edge until they see their prey and then the long neck shoots out and an unlucky fish is caught. Dippers are easily seen, hopping about on the stones in even the most turbulent streams, while the lucky visitor may even catch a glimpse of the brilliantly hued kingfisher. Sand martins, sandpipers, and wagtails all hunt their food in the river valleys.

Mammals

The pride of place must go to the sheep which, although domesticated to a degree, still live most of their lives roaming freely over the hills. The Swaledale ram, with its curled horns and black face was chosen as the most appropriate emblem for the Yorkshire Dales National Park.

Of the wholly wild life, the rabbit is almost as regularly met with as the sheep — the many that have fallen victim to the motor car are mute testimonies to their large numbers. Walkers in the grassland and on the moors will see them in rather livelier mood, though in recent years there has been a severe outbreak of myxomatosis. One of the sadder sights is a rabbit, panting beside a pathway unable to raise the strength to scuttle away from an

Rabbits are common in the region but, once again, they are threatened by myxomatosis.

advancing walker. The rabbit's enemies, the stoat and the weasel, are also common, sometimes in summer to be seen in pairs racing around the close-cropped grassland of the limestone country. The voles, field mice, and hedgehogs that are also numerous are less easily spotted.

The woodland offers shelter for the familiar sheep and rabbits, but there are still deer just as there were in the days of the old hunting forest. A patch of woodland, the Ingleton glens, is the one place where you can see that most charming of all woodland animals, the red squirrel. Another favourite animal, now sadly becoming rarer, is the otter, to be found on the Ure and the Wharfe.

The Dales offer a wonderfully rlch variety of animal life and if only the patient observer can expect to see some of the rarer species, everyone can enjoy the song of the birds. And the richness of the plant life, whether the purple heather of the moors or the sweet-smelling herbs of the pasture, create much of the special appeal of this unique area.

The weasel (left) can be seen on the hills, but it is largely nocturnal. The hedgehog (centre) can often be seen coming out to feed at dusk. The red squirrel (right) which, sadly, is now rare in England, still thrives in the Ingleton glens.

Leisure Activities

Useful Names and Addresses

TRANSPORT

Motoring
Automobile Association. Tel: (0532) 323999. Royal Automobile Club. Tel: (0532) 448556.

Bus, Coach, etc
Pennine Motor Services Company (075678) 215. Ribble Motor Services (0772) 54754. United Automobile Services Ltd (0325) 465252. West Yorkshire Road Car Company Ltd (0423) 66061. United Coaches (0904) 24161.

Train
Talking timetable: York-Leeds (0904) 37547. Leeds-York (0532) 449506. Harrogate-York (0423) 501372. Harrogate-Leeds (0423) 501371. Dales Rail — information at National Park Centres and Metro House, Wakefield. Ben Rhydding, Bingley, Burley-in-Wharfedale, Clapham, Crossflats, Dent, Gargrave, Garsdale, Giggleswick, Harrogate, Hellifield, Horton-in-Ribblesdale, Ilkley, Keighley, Kirkby Stephen, Long Preston, Pannal, Ribblehead, Settle: (0532) 448133. Knaresborough, Starbeck: (0904) 642155. Skipton (0756) 2543. York (0904) 642155.

Boat Trips and Cruises
Pennine Marine, Skipton (0756) 5478. Snaygill Boats, Skipton (0756) 5150. Castle Line, York (0904) 702240. Hills, York (0904) 425433. Ouse (0904) 425433. White Rose (0904) 28324. Lower Park Marina, Barnoldswick (0282) 815883.

Cycle Hire
Cycle Shop, The, Settle (07292)2216. Cyclists Touring Club (04868) 7217. Cobblestones Café, Grassington (0756) 752303. Dales Cycle Hire, Hawes (09679) 487. Freetime Activities, Sedbergh (05396) 20828. Kettlewell Garage, Kettlewell (075676) 225. Lyon Equipment, Dent (05875) 293. Mike Hogan Cycles, Skipton (0756) 4386. Sadlers, Thoralby (09693) 205. Thwaite Arms, Horsehouse (0969) 40206. Cycle Scene, York (0904) 53286. Rent-it, York (0904) 20173. Cycle Works, York (0904) 26664. Dial-a-Bike (0845) 567435. Cycling Holidays (0943) 862164.

LEISURE ACTIVITIES

Activity Centres
Baldersdale Youth Hostel (091284) 7473. Malham Tarn Field Studies Centre (07293) 331. Country Venture Activity Centre, Tebay (05874) 286. The Dales Centre, Grassington (0756) 752757. Whernside Manor Cave & Fell Centre (05875) 213.

Ballooning
Pennine Region Ballooning Association (0969) 40674. Balloon Flights Over the Yorkshire Dales (0756) 752937.

Camping and Caravanning
The Camping and Caravanning Club Ltd, Yorks Region (0472) 354558. The Caravan Club (0382) 26944. Yorkshire and *Humberside Caravan and Camping Guide* from the Tourist Board.

Canoeing
Barnard Castle Canoe Club (0833) 37829. British Canoe Union, Yorkshire and Humberside (0423) 330323.

Caving
Whernside Caving Centre (05875) 213.

Cycling
Cyclists Touring Club (0904) 769018. Yorkshire Dales Cycleway (130 miles), leaflets from Yorkshire Dales National Park. *Two Wheels* and *Mountain Bikeways* (Wharfedale and Craven areas) publications available from Embsay Steam Railway or Mike Hogan Cycles.

Fishing
Barnard Castle (0833) 31118. Salmon and Trout Association (0423) 862588. National Anglers' Council (0532) 440331. Yorkshire Water Authority (0532) 440191. North-west Water Authority Rivers Division (0925) 53999. *Anglers' Guide to North Yorkshire — Westmoreland Gazette*.

Gliding and Hang Gliding
Yorkshire Gliding Club (0485) 597237. British Hang Gliding Association (0937) 65587.

Golf
Barnard Castle Golf Club (0833) 38355. Barnoldswick (Ghyll) (028284) 2466. Catterick Garrison (0748) 833268. Harrogate (0423) 883485 (Crimple Valley); (0423) 863158/862999 (Harrogate); (0423) 67162 (Oakdale). Ilkley (0943) 608759 (Ben Rhydding); (0943) 600214/607277 (Ilkley). Knaresborough (0423) 863219. Masham (0765) 89379. Otley (0943) 465329. Richmond (0748) 2457. Ripon (0765) 3640 (Ripon City). Silsden (0535) 52998. Skipton (0756) 3257. York (0904) 413579 (Fulford); (0904) 424618 (Heworth); (0904) 706566 (Pike Hills); (0904) 490304 (York). Settle (07292) 2617.

Horse Racing

For all National Race Fixtures in Yorkshire (0765) 700698/690009 Catterick Bridge, Ripon, and York.

Lawn Tennis

Yorkshire Lawn Tennis Association (0274) 46242

Mountaineering

British Mountaineering Council Area Committee (0532) 742485

Orienteering

Yorkshire and Humberside Orienteering Association (0532) 505315

Parachuting and Parascending

British Association of Parascending Clubs (0533) 530318. British Parachute Association (0262) 678299.

Ramblers

North Yorkshire Ramblers Association.

Riding

British Horse Society (Yorks and Humberside) (0347) 21396. Riding for the Disabled (0677) 60231. Austwick (07292) 3214. Brough (09304) 651. Catterick (0748) 832521 ext. 2661. Coverdale (0969) 40668 and (0969) 40611. Eppleby (0325) 718286. Gargrave (075678) 243. Hawes (09697) 403. Kilnsey (0756) 752861. Reeth (0748) 84581. Swinton (0765) 89636. York (0904) 769029.

Rowing

Yorkshire and Humberside Rowing Council (075676) 810.

Sailing and Windsurfing

Royal Yachting Association (0482) 861585. Sports Council (0742) 747050.

Skiing

Yorkshire and Humberside Ski Federation (0274) 567402. Indoor ski centres at Catterick (0748) 833788. Harrogate (0423) 505457/8.

Sports Council Information Points

Harrogate (0423) 502744. Richmond (0748) 3120. Skipton (0609) 2926. York (0904) 54144.

Swimming Pools

Bingley (0274) 560621. Ilkley (0943) 600453. Ingleton (0468) 41049. Settle (0792) 3626. Threshfield (0756) 752261. York (0904) 30266; (0904) 793031; (0904) 22773.

Swimming Pools (Indoor) and Sports Centres

Grassington (0756) 752215. Harrogate (0423) 66282/883155. Richmond (0748) 4581. Ripon (0765) 3383. Settle (072 92) 3622. Skipton (0756) 2805.

Turkish Baths

Royal Baths, Harrogate (0423) 62498. White Wells Plunge Baths, Ilkley Moor (0943) 600066.

Walks

Information on guided walks is available from the National Park Centres or from their free newspaper *The Visitor*.

Information on walks and nature trails is also available from the National park Information Centres and includes trails such as the Malham Tarn Nature Trail, The Reginald Farrer Nature Trail, Hardraw Force and Ingleton Waterfalls Trail. There is also a Sedgewick Trail available from Sedbergh Tourist Information Centre.

Middleton Woods, Ilkley Moors, and River Wharfe Nature Trails prepared by Wharfedale Naturalists' Society available from Ilkley Tourist Information Centre.

Water Skiing

Barnard Castle Water Ski Club (0833) 50310. British Water Ski Federation (Yorks and Humberside) (0924) 253453.

Youth Hostels

The first number listed is the telephone number; the second is the number of the OS 1:25,000 map, followed by the map reference.

Aysgarth Falls (09693) 260; (98) 012884. Baldersdale (0833) 50629; (91,92) 931179. Earby (0282) 842349; (103) 915468. Ellingstring — (99) 176835; Lilac Cottage, Ellingstring, Ripon, North Yorks — no telephone; advance bookings and enquiries to: Yorkshire Area, 96 Main Street, Bingley BD16 2JH. Grinton Lodge (0748) 84206; (98) 048975. Hawes (09697) 368; (98) 867897. Ingleton (0468) 41444; (98) 695733. Keld (0748) 86259; (91,92) 891009. Kettlewell (075676) 232; (98) 970724. Kirkby Stephen (07683) 71793; (91) 774085. Linton (0756) 752400; (98) 998627. Malham (07293) 321; (98) 901629. Stainforth (07292) 3577; (98) 821668. York (0904) 653147; (105) 589528.

PLACES TO VISIT

Abbeys, Minsters, and Priories
Bolton Abbey (075671) 227. Coverham Abbey (0969) 40218. Easby Abbey (0748) 5224. Fountains Abbey and Studley Royal (076586) 333. Jervaulx Abbey (0677) 60226. Ripon Cathedral (0765) 2072. York Minster (0904) 624426.

Historic Houses, Castles, and Gardens
Braithwaite Hall (0969) 40287. Bolton Castle (0969) 23674. Broughton Hall (0756) 2267. Chapel and Coach House, Aske (0748) 3222. Constable Burton Hall Gardens (0677) 50361. Forcett Park (0325) 718226. Georgian Theatre Royal & Museum (0748) 3021. Harlow Car Gardens (0423) 65418. Markenfield Hall (0765) 2928. Middleham Castle (0969) 23899. Knaresborough Castle (0423) 503340. Newby Hall (0423) 322583. Parcevall Hall Gardens (075672) 311. Richmond Castle (0748) 2493. St Nicholas Gardens, Richmond (0748) 2328. Ripley Castle (0423) 770152. Rokeby Park (0833) 37334. Skipton Castle (0756) 2442. Spofforth Castle (0904) 22902.

York:
Assembly Rooms (0904) 59881. Clifford's Tower (0904) 646940. Fairfax House (0904) 55543. Guildhall (0904) 59881. King's Manor (0904) 59861. Merchant Adventurer's Hall (0904) 54518. Merchant Taylor's Hall (0904) 24889. Minster Library (0904) 25308. St Anthony's Hall (0904) 64315. St William's College (0904) 34830. Treasurer's House (0904) 24247. York House (0904) 86360.

Mills, Breweries, and Factories
High Corn Mill, Skipton (0756) 5521. Low Mill, Bainbridge (0969) 50416. W R Outhwaite & Son, Rope Factory, Hawes (09697) 487. Theakstons Brewery, Masham (0765) 89544.

Museums, Art Galleries, and Exhibitions
Bowes Museum (0833) 690606. Brontë Parsonage Museum, Haworth (0535) 42323. Craven Museum, Skipton (0756) 4079. Earby Mines Museum (0282) 843210. Green Howards Museum, Richmond (0748) 2133. Harrogate Art Gallery (0423) 503340. Manor House, Ilkley (0943) 600066. Museum of North Craven Life (07292) 2854. Nidderdale Museum, Pateley Bridge (0423) 711225. Old Courthouse Museum, Knaresborough (0423) 503340. Otley Museum (0943) 461052. RAF Regiment Museum, Catterick (0748) 811441. Richmondshire Museum, Richmond (0748) 5611. Ripon Prison and Police Museum (0765) 3706. Royal Pump Room Museum, Harrogate (0423) 503340. Swaledale Folk Museum, Reeth (0748) 84373. Upper Dales Folk Museum, Hawes (09697) 494. Upper Wharfedale Museum, Grassington (0756) 752800. Yorkshire Museum of Carriages and Horsedrawn Vehicles, Aysgarth (09693) 652. York Art Gallery (0904) 23834. York Castle Museum (0904) 53611. York Mansion House (0904) 59881. Yorkshire Museum, York (0904) 29475. Yorkshire Museum of Farming (0904) 489966. York Photographic Gallery (0904) 54724. York Story (0904) 28632.

Natural Attractions
Brimham Rocks (0423) 780688. How Stean Gorge, Lofthouse (0423) 75666. Ingleborough Show Cave, Clapham (04685) 242. Malham Tarn (07293) 416. Old Mother Shipton's Cave and Petrifying Well (0423) 864600. Stump Cross Caverns (0423) 711042. White Scar Caves, Ingleton (0468) 41244.

Preserved Steam Railways
Keighley and Worth Valley Railway (0535) 45214. Settle and Carlisle Railway (0228) 44711. Yorkshire Dales Railway (0756) 4727.

Tourist Information Centres
Barnard Castle (0833) 690000. Brough (09304) 260. Harrogate (0423) 525666. Hawes (09697) 450. Horton-in-Ribblesdale (07296) 333. Ilkley (0943) 602319. Ingleton (0468) 41049/41280. Kirkby Lonsdale (0468) 71603. Kirkby Stephen (07683) 71199. Knaresborough (0423) 866886. Leyburn (0969) 23069. Otley (0943) 465151. Pateley Bridge (0423) 711147. Reeth (0748) 84373. Richmond (0748) 850252. Ripon (0765) 4625. Scotch Corner (0748) 4864/2943. Sedbergh (05396) 20125. Settle (07292) 3617. Skipton (0756) 2809. York (0904) 21756/21757 or (0904) 643700.

National Park Information Centres
Aysgarth Falls (09693) 424. Clapham (04685) 419. Grassington (0756) 752748. Hawes (09697) 450. Malham (07293) 363. Sedbergh (05396) 20125.

National Park Information Points
Askrigg, Wensleydale Craft Shop. Bolton Abbey, The Post Office. Buckden, Riverside Gallery. Burnsall, The Post Office. Dent, Stone Close Café. Garsdale, Hive Garage/The Post Office. Gunnerside, The Post Office. Hebden, The Post Office. Horsehouse, The Post Office. Horton-in-Ribblesdale, Pen-y-Ghent Café. Kettle-

well, The Post Office. Kilnsey, Kilnsey Park Aquarium. Langcliffe, The Post Office. Litton, The Post Office. Muker, village store. Reeth, Swaledale Folk Museum. Stump Cross, Stump Cross Caverns. Thoralby, The Post Office.

Information

All national park information services may be identified by this symbol — look out for it when travelling through the Dales.

Yorkshire Dales National Park

Useful Telephone Numbers

Countryside Commission (Yorks & Humberside) (0532) 742935. Cumbria Tourist Board (09662) 4444. Field Studies Council, Malham Tarn (07293) 331. National Trust (0904) 659050. Nature Conservancy Council (North-east England) (0969) 23447. York Archaeological Trust (0904) 643211. Yorkshire Dales National Park (0756) 752748. Yorkshire Dales Society (0943) 607868. Yorkshire and Humberside Tourist Board (0904) 707961. Yorkshire Wildlife Trust (0904) 659570.

Emergency Information

Dental Emergency (0904) 30371. Hospitals (24-hour casualty): Duchess of Kent Military, Catterick (0748) 834397. Harrogate District (0423) 885959. Ripon and District (0765) 2546. York District (0904) 31313.

Weather (0898) 500417/418.

Further Useful Information

Early Closing Days:
TUESDAY Gargrave, Hellifield, Skipton. WEDNESDAY Harrogate, Hawes, Ilkley, Kirkby Lonsdale, Leyburn, Middleham, Otley, Richmond, Ripon, Settle, York. THURSDAY Appletreewick, Barnard Castle, Brough, Burnsall, Grassington, Hebden, Ingleton, Kettlewell, Kirkby Stephen, Knaresborough, Masham, Pateley Bridge, Reeth, Sedbergh.

Market Days:
MONDAY Hellifield, Kirkby Stephen. TUESDAY Hawes, Settle. WEDNESDAY Barnard Castle, Knaresborough, Masham, Sedbergh. THURSDAY Kirkby Lonsdale. FRIDAY Ingleton, Leyburn, Otley. SATURDAY Skipton official but Mon, Wed, Fri.

Mountain Rescue Posts — Dial 999
Aysgarth, Clapham, Grassington, Marske, Masham, Sedbergh, Settle.

Places of Interest

*Stars (★) after a place name indicate that the
place is featured elsewhere in this section.*

Appersett (98) (SD 8691) 1 mile NW of Hawes
This tiny hamlet huddled at the confluence of
Widdale Beck with the River Ure has an ancient
history. This was originally the Upper Seter of
the Norsemen, the summer farm, from which
they tended the flocks and herds. On **Tour 4.**

Appletreewick (98) (SE 0560) 4 miles SE of
Grassington
The village is centred on its steep, main street
climbing from Low Hall at one end to High Hall
at the other. Today it is a peaceful Wharfedale
village, but historically it was a place of importance. Bolton Priory ★ a little further down the
valley, acquired the manor which included good
grazing land and lead mines. In 1311 a charter
was granted for a fair to be held, known as the
Onion Fair, though now the only reminder of this
once important event is Onion Lane.

Appletreewick's most famous inhabitant was
the 'Dick Whittington of the Dales', Sir William
Craven. As a farmer's son he was sent to London
to make his fortune, which he duly achieved and
became Lord Mayor in 1610. He did not forget
his old home. He bought and rebuilt High Hall,
which is still standing, and endowed a grammar
school at nearby Burnsall ★. The cottage where
he was born is believed to have been one of the
pair which, in 1897-98, were converted to make
the church of St John. Mock Beggar Hall, or
Monk's Hall, as it is now usually known, stands
on the site of the Priory Grange and is a fine
house, mostly rebuilt at the end of the seventeenth century.

Arncliffe (98) (SD 9371) 6 miles NW of Grassington
The village lies at the heart of one of the loveliest
of the dales, Littondale, and is a suggested
stopping place for a stroll. It is visited on **Tour**

2. At its heart lies a wide green, surrounded by
mellow stone buildings with stone slate roofs.
Among these is the little Falcon Inn. Arncliffe is
a typical working community, with large porched
barns interspersed with the houses. Briefly, the
village joined the industrial revolution: a cotton
mill employing fifty workers was established
here in 1793, and the remains of the four-storey
building can be seen, now converted into flats,
at the far end of the green.

The church of St Oswald lies close to the
bridge over the Skirfare. It has a fine setting, but
most of the original architecture fell prey to
nineteenth-century 'restorers', though it still
boasts a memorial list of the Arncliffe men who
fought at Flodden in 1513. Across the bridge is
the house, Bridge End, where Charles Kingsley
was a frequent visitor and where he wrote much
of *The Water Babies*.

Askrigg (98) (SD 9491) 4 miles NW of Aysgarth
This ancient village was already well established as 'Ascric' by the time Domesday Book
came to be written, but it owes much of its present tourist popularity to television. Cringley
House on the market square became 'Skeldale
House' in the popular series based on James
Herriot's stories of his life as a country vet. But
the village would be well worth visiting for its
own sake. It was granted a market charter in
1587, but it seems to have functioned as an un-
official trading centre long before that. The
market cross is still the focal point, and, nearby
set into the cobbles, is the iron ring to which
bulls were tethered for baiting. Near the cross is
the beautiful fifteenth-century church, with its
tall tower, broad nave, and fine nave roof, a tes-
tament to the town's former importance.

Askrigg's market went into decline when a
new turnpike road through Hawes ★ was built
to the south of the River Ure. There was, however, continued prosperity based on clock
making, cotton spinning and dyeing, and knitting. This is reflected in the many handsome
eighteenth- and early nineteenth-century houses
in the town. The routing of the turnpike may
have seemed bad news at the time but now it
seems a blessing. Quietly settled away from the
main road, it has been spared the rush of heavy
traffic and development, and its special character should now be preserved for it has recently
been given Conservation Area status.

Askrigg is visited on **Tour 6** and is one of the

places suggested for a stroll. A path leading westwards from the church takes you to the beautiful 24-ft high Mill Gill waterfall and, beyond that, to Whitfield Gill Force which is not so easy to see from the stroll. The outstanding building of the area is Nappa Hall 1½ miles to the east on the Woodhall road. It is not open to the public but can be seen clearly from the road. Nappa Hall is a fifteenth-century fortified farmhouse with a single-storey hall flanked by battlemented towers.

Austwick (98) (SD 7668) 4 miles NW of Settle
This pleasantly unpretentious village, just north of the A65, dates back to the Norsemen who named it the Aust Wick or eastern settlement. It has a village green and a market cross, which has been restored as a reminder of former glories before the market moved on to nearby Clapham ★. Austwick's present claim to fame lies just outside the village, the Norber Boulders. There is a pleasant stroll from Town Head northwards up to Norber Hill, or it is possible to drive up Crummack Lane. The Boulders are more properly known to geologists as the Norber Erratics, huge rocks that were brought down by the glaciers. The limestone around them eroded away, leaving them standing high above the ground on little platforms and pedestals.

Aysgarth (98) (SE 0088) 7 miles W of Leyburn
This is one of the most popular spots in the Dales, not because of the village itself but because of its famous waterfalls. The village lies on the A684, but most visitors will want to turn off on the minor road to the east of the village, between the Palmer Flatt Hotel and the youth hostel. This leads past the church of ancient foundation, but now mainly Victorian aspect,

James Herriot

No writer of this century has done more to illuminate the Dales and their traditional farms, not to mention their often idiosyncratic farmers, than James Herriot. A country vet is not perhaps the likeliest candidate for literary fame, but then neither was a trio of poor parson's daughters, and Herriot's stories had achieved immense popularity long before television made them, and the actors who portray the characters, known to millions. There is an area of the Dales which takes in some of its most beautiful scenery — Swaledale, Wensleydale, and Coverdale — which, for his many admirers, is simply Herriot Country.

Herriot's success is based on apparently simple stories, the chronicling of the life of a country vet. But there is far more to it than that. What he has done is capture the essence of a particular place at a particular time. He knew and recorded the life of the Dales at a time when the heavy horse was as common as the tractor is today, when tradition was not a set of quaint customs preserved for visitors

but a living part of everyday life. Most importantly of all, he conveyed his love of the Dales countryside — not the admiration of a visitor, but the much deeper feelings of a man who knows it intimately in all seasons and all moods.

The popular television series, All Creatures Great and Small, used locations well known to Herriot. Many scenes were shot in and around Reeth, where the unit was based, and, if you wish to identify the narrow tortuous road along which the car trundles at the start of each episode, then travel up Arkengarthdale, and a ½mile past Langthwaite, turn left on the road signposted to Low Row. The veterinary practice was located, for the filming, in Askrigg, and Bedale and Leyburn were also regularly featured. But there is no need diligently to search out television locations to get a feel for Herriot country: it is there in every traditional village, each busy market town, and, more than anywhere else, it can be found in the isolated farms or remote valleys and high moors.

horsedrawn vehicles. It also has a viewing platform from which to see the Falls.

Bainbridge (98) (SD 9390) 4 miles east of Hawes
This is a village of great charm and interest that straddles the A684, and features on **Tour 5**. The central feature is the vast village green, with its old stocks and the Rose and Crown which, although it dates back to 1443, was much altered when the turnpike road was built down Wensleydale, to take advantage of the new coaching trade. Here they keep the horn which is still blown each winter evening at nine o'clock to guide travellers to safety. The custom goes back to the days when Bainbridge was surrounded by forest, and the original horn can be seen in the museum at Castle Bolton ★. At the eastern end of the village, the road crosses the River Bain which splashes through in a series of little waterfalls on its way down from Semer Water ★. There is a pleasant walk up the side of the river which is included as part of **Walk 7**. Beyond the

across the narrow stone bridge to the National Park Centre and car park. This features on **Tour 5**. Here you can stop for a short walk to see the falls. There are three sets of falls altogether, which carry the River Ure down over a series of ledges. To see them all you follow the well-signposted footpath through Freeholders' Wood.
Yore Mill, by the bridge, has had a very mixed history. It was built in 1784 as a worsted mill, converted to spinning cotton, and rebuilt in 1850 after a fire. It was then used as a woollen mill whose output included red cloth which went to make shirts for Garibaldi's army. When the textile trade died away, it was converted to a grain mill and is now the Yorkshire Carriage Museum with a collection of more than sixty

The ruins of Barden Tower. This was the favourite home of Lady Anne Clifford.

bridge, on the left, is a small hill which was the site of the Roman fort of Virosidum, and the Roman road which can be easily seen to the south-east also features on **Walk 7**.

Bank Newton (103) (SD 9153) 5 miles W of Skipton
A small hamlet, but an excellent spot to pause for a stroll along the Leeds and Liverpool Canal. There are six wide locks here, while, to the south, the canal twists and turns to thread its way through the hills in one of the most scenic reaches of the whole waterway. This is included on **Tour 2**.

Barbon (97) (SD 6282) 3 miles N of Kirkby Lonsdale
This pleasant village lies just to the east of the A683. It has a lovely Victorian church which is unusually restrained. The big east window has clear glass, the architect wisely deciding that the magnificent view through to the fells was preferable to stained glass. The pack-horse bridge crossing Barbon Beck is reached down the road opposite the Wesleyan chapel. **Tour 4** runs by the village on the main road.

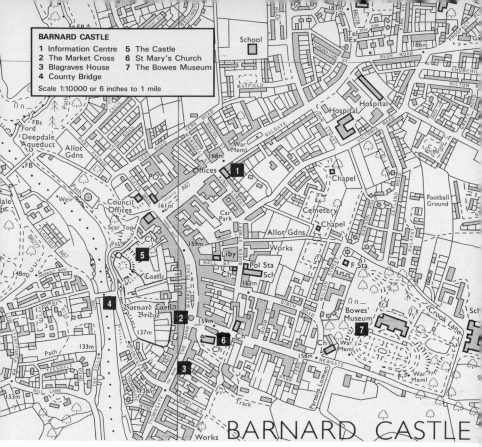

Barden Tower (104) (SE 0557) 4 miles NE of Skipton

The imposing ruin can be seen on the side of the B6160. It was begun in the eleventh century as a fortress from which the surrounding forest was administered. In 1310 it passed to the Clifford family, and Henry, the tenth Lord Clifford, lived here in preference to the grandeur of Skipton Castle ★, earning himself the name the 'Shepherd Lord'. It was repaired and improved by the great local benefactress, Lady Anne Clifford, in the seventeenth century, but was never lived in again after her death. Today it is a romantic ruin, but the adjoining priest's house and chapel are now a restaurant. Barden appears on **Tour 1** and **Walk 1**.

Barnard Castle (92) (NZ 0516)

The town grew up around the castle of Bernard de Baliol, whose father, Guy, fought with William the Conqueror at Hastings. The castle is still there, overlooking the river crossing, but no longer appears as a major feature in the town itself, for over the centuries, Barnard Castle has developed to become one of the most attractive market towns in the north of England. Its appeal derives in good measure from its situation standing on a high bank, with its main streets climbing up steeply from the River Tees. The town is also fortunate in possessing a wealth of solidly attractive buildings.

The starting point for any walk around the town has to be its most prominent feature, the Market Cross (2) that stands in the centre of the road at the bottom of the Market Place. This octagonal building was put up in 1747 as the Town Hall though produce was sold in the open colonnade. The road downhill is simply, but aptly named, The Bank, for it dives precipitously towards the river. It is lined by handsome stone town houses, including Blagraves House (3). The present building is early sixteenth century, but rests on earlier foundations and gets its name from the family who lived here in the seventeenth century. The most prominent feature is the four-storey bay. The rest of the building is a bit of a hotchpotch, with an eighteenth-century door up the steps and a Tudor door at street level, and with nineteenth-century carved musicians looking down on both. The street changes its name halfway down to Thorngate, and Thorngate House itself boasts a fine Georgian frontage.

At the riverside the whole atmosphere changes from market town to industrial centre. Here are memories of a once busy woollen industry with mills and weavers' cottages. At the foot of the street you can cross the Tees on a footbridge and look down on the river as it carves its way through limestone and marble. A short riverside walk now takes you to the road bridge (4), which was rebuilt in 1569 — not 1596 as a tablet at the eastern end has it. The rebuilding in fact followed a siege of the castle in that year. The castle (5) itself now appears at its most majestic,

35

rising above the high cliff, but this is also still the industrial area, and, just before you cross the bridge, you can see more weavers' cottages, with their tell-tale long windows on the upper floors to supply light for the looms.

The castle is not merely grand in itself but provides a magnificent viewpoint. The most prominent features are the fourteenth-century round tower and the remains of the fifteenth-century great chamber. In its day it was obviously a place of considerable size and importance, and can boast some suitably important owners. John Baliol had an argument with the Bishop of Durham and actually hit the cleric, for which he paid a penance: he established a hostel for poor students which eventually became Balliol College, Oxford. Warwick the King Maker lived here and it passed to his daughter who married Richard III. The king's emblem, the boar, can be seen on the wall of the great chamber.

From the castle you come out at the junction of Galgate and the Horse Market, the latter leading straight on into the Market Place. Down here are two notable inns: the seventeenth-century Golden Lion and the King's Head Hotel, where Dickens stayed while working on *Nicholas Nickleby*. The original Dotheboys Hall is nearby at Bowes ★. Just off the Market Place is St Mary's Church, which is basically Norman but with Victorian overtones.

There is one other important building in the town: the Bowes Museum **(7)**, a little to the east of the town centre, past the church down Newgate. It is a somewhat surprising building to find in a northern market town, for it looks for all the world like a French château. There is, however, a simple explanation. George Bowes, who had it built in the nineteenth century, was married to a French actress and employed a French architect. It now houses a most distinguished collection, including some very fine paintings, and all in a most sumptuous setting. **Tour 8** starts at Barnard Castle.

Not a French château, but the Bowes Museum at Barnard Castle.

Barningham (92) (NZ 0810) 4 miles SE of Barnard Castle
The village, through which **Tour 8** passes, is one of those rare places where all the elements seem to come together in pleasing harmony. There is a long, wide green bounded by stone cottages and houses, an attractive early nineteenth-century church, and the gateway to Barningham Park, all seen against a background of low, wooded hills.

Barnoldswick (103) (SD 8746) 7 miles SW of Skipton
A small industrial town, once in Yorkshire but now in Lancashire — though the Yorkshire County Cricket Club will still accept Barnoldswick players as Yorkshiremen regardless of Whitehall edicts. The Leeds and Liverpool Canal passes through the town, with the attractive Greenber Field locks lying just to the north off the B6252. Barnoldswick's modern claim to fame is as the research centre for Rolls Royce aero-engines.

Fewston reservoir on the River Washburn now seems almost to be a natural feature.

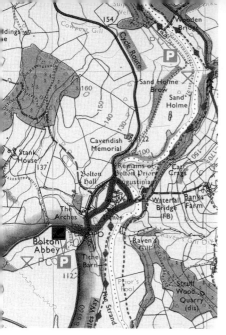

A view of Bolton Priory beside the River Wharfe. The river can be crossed by the bridge or by the stepping stones.

Beamsley (104) (SE 0752) 4 miles NW of Ilkley
A small but pleasing village that sits in the Wharfe valley below the steep slopes of Beamsley Beacon. To the north of the village on the A59 is a small group of almshouses, Beamsley Hospital on **Tour 1**, founded in 1593 by Margaret, Countess of Cumberland and developed by her daughter, Lady Anne Clifford. They look conventional from the main road, but through an arch one can see a circular stone building with a stone roof. It has a central chapel, with seven rooms for poor women radiating round it. It is now let as holiday accommodation.

Bewerley (99) (SE 1565) ½ mile SW of Pateley Bridge
The village looks across the Nidd to Pateley Bridge ★. Its principal attraction is the little chapel built in the sixteenth century by Marmaduke Huby, the last abbot of Fountains Abbey ★. The Hall, sadly, was demolished in 1926.

Blubberhouses (104) (SE 1755) 7 miles W of Harrogate
This tiny village, with a pretty little church, gives its name to the moors through which the busy A59, Skipton ★ to Harrogate ★ road passes. It stands on the River Washburn which has been dammed to create a series of reservoirs — Thruscross to the north, Fewston ★, Swinsty, and Lindley Wood to the south. On **Tour 1**.

Bolton Abbey (104) (SE 0754) 5 miles NW of Ilkley
Bolton Abbey is a tiny hamlet named after the beautiful Priory Church established by the Augustinians in the twelfth century. The buildings themselves are reached through Hole-in-the-

The gaunt keep of twelfth-century Bowes Castle stands high above the River Greta.

Wall, which is exactly what its name suggests. At once a splendid view opens out across a wide bend of the Wharfe, crossed by stepping stones. Then the Priory appears in view, with Bolton Hall alongside. The Hall was originally the Priory gateway but, at the Dissolution, Henry VIII sold the estate to the Earl of Cumberland for the odd sum of £2490. 1s. 1d, and he converted it into a hunting lodge. The church itself was more fortunate than many of the other great foundations in that the nave at least was preserved as the parish church. The rest of the church, even in its ruins, is quite magnificent, and is given true grandeur by the beauty of its setting. The Abbey is suggested as a stopping-off point for a stroll on **Tour 1**, and the more energetic can follow **Walk 1** up the river to the Strid, a narrow chasm through which the river forces its way in a thunderous cascade, and on to Barden Tower ★. A leaflet showing the route of a nature walk in the riverside woods is available from the park hut.

Bowes (92) (NY 9913) 4 miles SW of Barnard Castle
This is a quiet village with a wide main street, freed from traffic by the A66 bypass. It has two claims to fame. The elder of the two is the castle,

O, Brignal banks are wild and fair
And Greta woods are green.

There are footpaths along both banks of the river. The north bank is most easily approached from Greta Bridge ★, after a walk of about 1½ miles. There is a short path to the south bank from Scargill, past Scargill Castle, but motorists should note that parking near Scargill is very difficult to find. Greta Bridge and Scargill are both on **Tour 8**.

Brimham Rocks (99) (SE 2165) 8 miles SW of Ripon, off B6265

The rocks are gritstone outcrops spread over a wide area of high moorland with superb views out across Nidderdale, all the way to the distant towers of York Minster. Wind, rain, and frost have eaten away at the stone to create fantastical shapes which, as their different names indicate, can suggest anything from a kissing chair to a dancing bear. They are now in the care of the National Trust, which provides an information centre in Brimham House — rebuilt in 1780 from an older house. The whole area in the Trust's care extends over 387 acres and it has been suggested for a stroll, featured on **Tour 9**.

a gaunt, uncompromising keep built in the twelfth century as a defence against the Border raiders coming down from Scotland. The site overlooking the River Greta was earlier taken by the Romans for their fort of Lavatris. At the western end of the village is Dotheboys Hall, now subdivided into houses. Dickens came here in 1838 and used it as the basis for Wackford Squeers' atrocious school in *Nicholas Nickleby*. Bowes can be found on **Tour 8**.

Brignall Banks (92) (NZ 0511) 3 miles S of Barnard Castle

The banks are the beautiful wooded banks of the River Greta to the west of Greta Bridge ★. They were praised in Sir Walter Scott's *Rokeby*.

Brough (91) (NY 7914) 4 miles N of Kirkby Stephen

Brough consists of two parts, separated by the A66: Market Brough to the north and Church Brough to the south, each with its own very distinctive character.

Market Brough's trading role is plain from its wide main street, with its 1911 clock tower incorporating part of the original market cross. There has been a major trans-Pennine road through here since Roman times, and the town enjoyed some prosperity in the coaching days of the eighteenth and nineteenth centuries, though some of its old inns are now private houses. Across the river close to the bridge is the handsome former Quaker Meeting House.

Where Market Brough is based on a long, wide main street, Church Brough is more like an

Looking down over the village of Church Brough from the ramparts of Brough Castle built by the Normans on the site of a Roman fort.

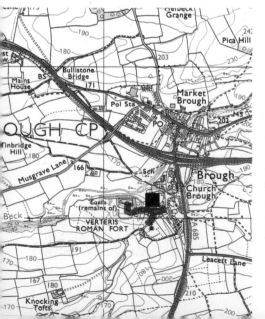

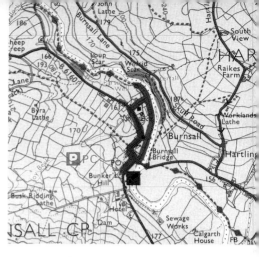

intimate village arranged around a central square. On **Tour 7** there is a recommendation that visitors park here for a walk round the village and to visit Brough Castle. This is a somewhat curious building. Like other northern fortresses, such as Bowes ★, this was a Norman castle built on the site of a Roman fort, but it was badly damaged by fire in 1521 and the indomitable Lady Anne Clifford set about rebuilding it in suitably Gothic style in the seventeenth century. Much of what is on view today shows the results of the restoration she inaugurated. It is still grandly impressive, as is the little church which still retains many Norman features and has a somewhat macabre, barred squint-hole near the altar.

Buckden (98) (SD 9477) 4 miles N of Kettlewell
The village stands near the northern end of Wharfedale, just before the point where it turns sharply to the west to acquire the name, Langstrothdale. It is an important site, and the village more than meets the challenge. The Buck Inn is not just a play on words, for the village was established as a hunting centre for Norman lords who pursued the deer of Langstrothdale Chase. The present-day village, with its neat green, shows that uniformity of style which gives it away as an estate village, owing its prosperity to the local hall, Buckden House, now a holiday home for Methodists.

Burley in Wharfedale (104) (SE 1646) 2 miles E of Ilkley
Burley is very typical of the small towns of this end of Wharfedale, a place of solid, robust character, lacking the very obvious charms of the villages of the upper dales. Its character comes largely from the stone that can be seen lining the edge of the moorland above the town, the dark, almost black, gritstone. This stone inevitably gives the houses built from it a somewhat dour

The village of Burnsall stretches along the banks of the Wharfe.

appearance. Yet the town, with its old mills, belongs securely in this landscape, and is a spot of good, honest buildings in a dramatic setting between the river and the craggy moors.

Burnsall (98) (SE 0361) 3 miles SE of Grassington
Burnsall is everything a Dales village should be. Its shape is dictated by the landscape, the long village street winding its way to follow the line of the Wharfe, opening out where space allows into a tree-shaded green. The houses are of rich, warm stone, many dating back to the seventeenth century and showing the typical small, mullioned windows of the period. All around are the fells, to the north showing the white scars of limestone cliffs, while, to the south, the darker, harder edges of gritstone dominate the valley. There are signs of old settlements in the village church. The present building was begun in the twelfth century and was largely rebuilt in the sixteenth, but it stands on the site of a much earlier foundation. There are Norse crosses of the ninth and tenth centuries, and gravestones from the same period, but the church's chief glory is the medieval Adoration of the Magi,

Fourteenth-century Bolton Castle.

carved from alabaster. There is also a tablet to the 'Dick Whittington of the Dales', Sir William Craven of Appletreewick ★ , who repaired the church, and endowed the grammar school, which still stands by the church, though now it is a primary school. The church also has an unusual lychgate with a seventeenth-century turnstile mechanism.

Burnsall's busiest day of the year comes on the Saturday following the first Sunday after 12 August, when the classic fell race is run — the oldest in the county. Burnsall is a recommended stopping point on **Tour 1**, and visitors can stroll out on to the fellside — which at least gives some idea of the effort needed to run up it.

The deep pot holes of Butter Tubs Pass.

Burton in Lonsdale (97) (SD 6572) 3 miles W of Ingleton
This village on the A687 stands just on the Yorkshire side of the county border with Lancashire by a bridge over the River Greta. Once there was a small castle here, the town received a charter to hold a market in 1274, and, in its time, it was famous for its potteries. Now it is a pleasant, quiet village.

Butter Tubs Pass (98) (SD 8796) 4 miles N of Hawes on road to Muker
The pass climbs to a height of 1726 feet and gets its name from pot holes on either side of the road approximately 1/2 mile short of the summit on the Hawes ★ side. The name is thought to derive from the habit of local farmers, taking butter to market, who paused here to give their pack animals a rest. They were said to have lowered their butter into the dark depths to keep it cool. Or perhaps the limestone pillars that separate the holes look like old-style butter tubs. The holes themselves are deep and should be approached with caution. The pot holes feature on **Tour 5**.

Carlton (99) (SE 0684) 4 miles SW of Leyburn
This is the principal village in the beautiful and lonely valley of Coverdale, featured on **Tour 3**. It is a long, straggling village, with few pretensions but possessing a quiet, dignified charm. It

has, however, its own Bard, Henry Constantine, whose verses may long since have been forgotten by all but locals, but passers-by can still read eight of his lines inscribed over the doorway of the Georgian vicarage where he lived. Carlton is, like the whole dale, a place of quiet charms which never even had a made-up road until World War II.

Carperby (98) (SE 0089) 1 mile N of Aysgarth
This long Wensleydale village, stretching for ½ mile down the road was granted a market charter in 1303. The only reminder of those days is the impressive seventeenth-century market cross. It has a friendly village inn, the Wheatsheaf, where the Herriots spent their honeymoon. Its other claim to fame can be seen on the surrounding hills, an extensive system of strip lynchets, the cultivation platforms carved out of the slope by medieval farmers. Carperby features on **Tour 5**.

Casterton (97) (SD 6279) 1 mile N of Kirkby Lonsdale
This little village of grey stone houses huddles down under the shelter of the hills above the River Lune. Charlotte Brontë was at a School for Clergymen's Daughters in Cowan Bridge ★ from 1824 to 1825. The school was later moved to Casterton and became Casterton School. She used it in *Jane Eyre*. Brontë House, across the road from the church, was originally the Servants' School. Casterton lies on **Tour 4**.

Castle Bolton (98) (SE 0391) 5 miles W of Leyburn
Castle Bolton is, not surprisingly, the small village that grew up alongside Bolton Castle. The castle was built by Lord Scrope, a friend of Richard II, as an imposing quadrangular fortress with towers at each corner. Work began in 1378, and local legend has it that ox blood was mixed with the mortar to give added strength. It would seem to have succeeded, for the castle is remarkably well preserved, though there has been a good deal of restoration work. Mary Queen of Scots stayed here for six months in 1568 following her defeat by the Protestant forces, and her room has been refurbished. After the Civil War the castle was, by order, left untenanted for 300 years. Today, visitors can enjoy the building for itself and for the magnificent views from its battlements.
 The village was established at the same time as the castle and is a pleasant spot with wide greens and an attractive fourteenth-century church. On **Tour 5**.

Catterick Garrison (99) (SE 1897) 2 miles S of Richmond
This huge army camp has a special place in the memories of a whole generation who began their National Service here. Their grumbles at the seemingly endless days of drill were no doubt echoing those of soldiers of nearly 2,000 years earlier, for Cataractonium was a Roman legionary camp named after the cataracts or waterfalls on the Swale. The Roman camp was

The 600-foot waterfall, Cautley Spout.

3 miles to the east of where modern Catterick stands.

Cautley Spout (98) (SD 6897) 3 miles N of Sedbergh
This waterfall on the flank of Howgill Fells has an unbroken fall of 600 feet. It can be approached by a footpath from the Cross Keys Inn on the A683 between Sedbergh ★ and Kirkby Stephen ★. Those expecting to stop here for a glass of ale will, however, be disappointed for this old inn is a temperance house in the care of the National Trust. This is a suggested stopping place on **Tour 7**. It is slightly over ½ mile to the fall, which is clearly visible on the fellside.

Chapel-le-Dale (98) (SD 7477) 4 miles NE of Ingleton
This is a tiny village in a dramatic setting,

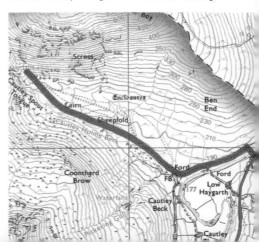

Down the valley from below Cautley Spout.

squeezed into the narrow valley between the heights of Whernside and Ingleborough. A Roman road came this way and, more recently, the railway arrived, cutting across the head of the valley on the great Ribblehead Viaduct. The church of St Leonard has a memorial plaque to the 200 men, women, and children who died in the nearby shanty towns during the building of the Settle and Carlisle railway — mostly from disease. The little village churchyard had to be enlarged to take the graves. Car parking is available by the Old Hill Inn on the main B6255 road. This is the starting place for **Walk 5** on **Tour 4**.

Church Brough (see Brough)

Clapham (98) (SD 7469) 6 miles NW of Settle
The village has now, mercifully, been bypassed by the A65, leaving Clapham tucked peacefully away in a wooded valley below Ingleborough. Much of the character of the village derives from the Farrer family who settled here in the eighteenth century, rebuilt Ingleborough Hall, developed Clapham as an estate village, and altered the surrounding landscape by damming Clapham beck to create a lake and filling the Clapham Gill with trees. The beck does, however, still run through the village, where it is crossed by four bridges.

Clapham is a favourite centre for potholers, but non-experts also have a chance to see something of the underground system of caves. A nature trail starts at the National Park Information Centre, where there is a car park. The trail, named after the botanist Reginald Farrer, takes you to Ingleborough Cave, where there are conducted tours. The really adventurous can be taken for an exploration of Gaping Gill, organised by the Craven Pothole Club, Clapdale Woods. This vast cavern has a main chamber big enough to hold York Minster. Clapham has the distinction of being home to the highly successful local magazine, *The Dalesman*.

Conistone (98) (SD 9867) 2 miles NW of Grassington
This tiny Wharfedale village nestles under the lee of limestone crags and looks out across the valley to the overhanging cliffs above Kilnsey ★. An old stone bridge crosses the river and the Norman church still retains its original arcading. On **Tour 3**.

Constable Burton Hall (99) (SE 1691) 3½ miles E of Leyburn
Constable Burton Hall is a fine Palladian House of 1762. Although it is not open to the public, the park is. It is a fine example of an informal Georgian garden with flower beds, a lake, and pleasant strolls among the trees. The entrance is on the A684.

Countersett (98) (SD 9187) 5 miles E of Hawes
The hamlet perches on top of a steep hill above the northern end of Semer Water ★. A quiet place of old stone houses, it has just one especially fine house, Countersett Hall. Its most famous occupant was Richard Robinson who, in the seventeenth century, established the Quaker faith in Wensleydale. **Tour 5** and **Walk 7** pass through Countersett.

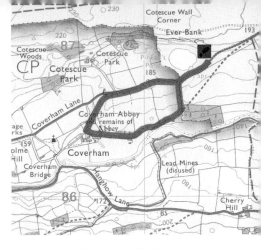

Coverham (99) (SE 1086) 3 miles S of Leyburn
This little village sits near the beginning of beautiful Coverdale. The 'White Canons' founded an abbey at Swainby in Swaledale in the twelfth century, but stayed there for only twenty-five years. There was an argument with Ranulph Fitzrobert, the son of the foundress, so a new site was found in Coverdale. Not a great deal now remains of Coverham Abbey, much of the stone having been robbed to build the village houses, and part has been absorbed into the Georgian house by the site. There is enough left, however, to give an impression of the size and importance of the foundation.

The village is a place of quiet charms, with a simple church, a little mill house, and a single-arched medieval bridge over the Cover, probably built by the monks. This is a suggested stopping place for a stroll on **Tour 3**.

Cowan Bridge (97) (SD 6477) 2 miles SE of Kirkby Lonsdale
The village takes its name from the bridge over the Leck beck. In January 1824, the Reverend Carus Wilson opened a school in converted cottages. Maria and Elizabeth Brontë came as boarders in July of that year, to be followed in the autumn by Charlotte and Emily. The conditions were bad and the regime harsh, and the girls were soon removed. The school appears as 'Lowood' in *Jane Eyre* and it is identified by a wall plaque alongside the A65. **Tour 4** passes through the village.

Cray (98) (SD 9479) 4½ miles N of Kettlewell
This hamlet is easily missed for it lies on a dead-end road just off the B6160, near Hubberholme ★. There is not very much to it — a few stone houses and an inn — but it has a most beautiful setting at the end of Bishopdale, and there is an impressive waterfall just above Cray High Bridge to the north of the village. It is on **Tour 6** and **Walk 10**.

From the path to Ingleborough Cave to the harsh outline of the limestone escarpment.

Dent (98) (SD 7086) 4 miles SE of Sedbergh
If there was a competition held to find the most attractive village in the Dales, then Dent would be a finalist. If there were another contest to find the least accessible, then Dent would do equally well. The two are not unconnected. Dent, with its whitewashed stone houses and narrow cobbled streets, is the very model of an unspoiled village, quiet and peaceful, removed from the rush and bustle of the rest of the world. It was not always so. This was the capital of the ancient but tiny Kingdom of Dent. In its day it was famous for its marble quarries, and examples of local marble can be seen on the floor of the fifteenth-century church. The industry declined and then disappeared in the late nineteenth century. The other local occupation was knitting: the locals became known as 'the terrible knitters of Dent', not a criticism of their craft but a comment on the furious rate at which they worked. Local knitwear is still on sale in the village.

In the centre of the village is a slab of Shap granite, a memorial to Adam Sedgwick, a native of Dent who went on to become Professor of Geology at Cambridge.

Dent is a place to linger and relax, but those who want to explore the dale can take **Walk 6**. **Tour 4** passes through the village.

Earby (103) (SD 9046) 6 miles SW of Skipton
Earby stands just over the county border in Lancashire, but is home to the Yorkshire Dales Lead Mining Museum. This was established by the Earby Mines Research Group, local potholers who have been involved in exploration and restoration work. The museum, housed in the old Grammar School in School Lane, shows the results of their work in photographs and in the artefacts they have retrieved.

The ruins of the White Canons abbey at Easby beside the River Swale.

Easby (92) (NZ 1800) 1 mile SE of Richmond
Here, in a pleasant riverside setting, are the remains of Easby Abbey. Like Coverham ★, this was a Premonstratensian abbey of the White Canons but, unlike Coverham, a good deal has survived and is now in the care of English Heritage. The gatehouse has scarcely been altered since the fourteenth century, while the refectory

The Descent from the Cross, a thirteenth-century fresco in Easby church.

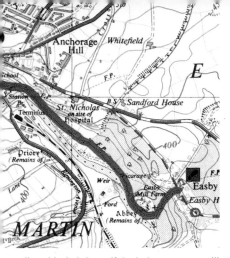

East Witton was a market town in the fourteenth century but is now reduced to one street, rebuilt in 1809, as the stone records.

walls, with their beautiful window tracery, still rise to their full height. The Abbey was founded by Roalbus, Constable of Richmond ★ in 1152, but the parish church is slightly earlier. There was a magnificent Anglo-Saxon cross here, but it was taken away to the Victoria and Albert Museum in London, and a replica stands in its place. The thirteenth-century frescoes, however, can still be seen in situ. They show a whole range of subjects including the passing of the seasons as well as the usual Biblical stories. Easby is a stopping place on **Tour 8**, for a stroll round the ancient buildings or along the riverside walk to Richmond.

East Marton (103) (SD 9050) 5 miles W of Skipton
This little village, with its isolated church, sits astride the A59 but also, rather more interestingly, the Leeds and Liverpool Canal. The canal bridge is a most unusual double-arched affair — the arches not conventionally side by side, but one on top of the other. The bridge was raised

and this was the easiest way to do it. The conjunction of main road and canal accounts for the unusually large pub by the bridge. The surrounding countryside undulates with green hillocks, around which the canal snakes in extravagant bends, especially in the section to the north leading up to Bank Newton ★. The Pennine Way uses the towpath through the village.

East Witton (99) (SE 1486) 3 miles SE of Leyburn
The village has known better times. In 1306 it had a market charter and, by the end of the century, there were over 200 tax-payers. Now it has been reduced to just one tree-lined street, rebuilt in 1809 by the Earl of Ailesbury who also gave it the dignified Regency church. Nearby, a mile to the north, on the road to Spennithorne ★ is Ulshaw Bridge, which has a sundial in the cutwater dated 1674 — a time check for travellers. On **Tour 3**.

Braithwaite Hall, between Coverham and East Witton, is a fine seventeenth-century house.

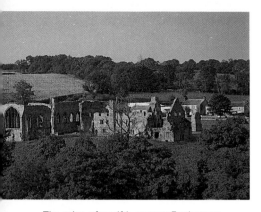

The ruins of twelfth-century Egglestone Abbey. The buildings to the right were converted into a house at the Dissolution.

Egglestone Abbey (92) (NZ 0615) 1 mile SE of Barnard Castle
The abbey ruins stand in a lovely situation close by the old bridge over the Tees. Like others in the area, this was a Premonstratensian foundation of the twelfth century, and it still retains much of its former grandeur. The cruciform church still has nave and chancel walls standing, and the chancel, with its Early English lancet windows, is particularly fine. The other buildings were converted into a house after the Dissolution, and still have typical Tudor mullioned windows. The churchyard is well worth exploring for the carved medieval gravestones.

Embsay (104) (SE 0153) 2 miles NE of Skipton
This village of dark stone houses sits under the shadow of Embsay Moor and looks out on the raw scars left by quarrying on Haw Park Hill. It was originally served by the Midland Railway line from Skipton ★ to Ilkley ★, but that closed in 1965. Now it has been reopened by enthusiasts as the Yorkshire Dales Railway, running steam trains from Embsay Station on part of the old track. Eventually it is hoped to reopen the route all the way to Bolton Abbey ★. Opposite the station a minor road climbs steeply up the hill past an old textile mill. The mill pond, now home to ducks and swans, stands next to a delightful stone house of 1665. (See **Tour 2**).

Eshton (103) (SD 9356) 1 mile N of Gargrave
This is a tiny hamlet, but it is memorable because the minor road from Gargrave ★ to Malham ★ passes through the middle of the splendid parkland of Eshton Hall. This was the home of the Wilson family who acquired the estate in the seventeenth century and built the present handsome mansion in the 1820s. It is now a private home for the elderly.

Feetham and Low Row (98) (SD 9898) 3 miles W of Reeth
These two villages now join together as a long straggle of houses down the B6270. It seems to have little significance now, but once it was a resting place on the Corpse Way (see Grinton ★). The seventeenth-century Punch Bowl Inn must have been a welcome sight for the pall bearers coming down the valley or over the

fells. It might be equally welcome — if for less macabre reasons — to visitors on **Tour 6**.

Fewston (104) (SE 1954) 6 miles N of Otley
Fewston is known as 'the moving village' because of subsidence. It could equally well be the fiery village, because its first two churches burned down. The present building dates from 1697. Today the village sits between two reservoirs, with pleasant wooded banks. **Tour 1** crosses between the two artificial lakes and you can stop at the car park at the southern end for a stroll through the woods to the dam.

Fountains Abbey (99) (SE 2768) 3 miles SW of Ripon, off the B6265
The Abbey of St Mary of the Fountains was established in the twelfth century by a group of monks who felt that life at St Mary's Abbey in York had become too soft and corrupt. So they settled in the deep, wooded valley of the River Skell, described by a contemporary as 'more fit, it seemed, for the lair of wild beasts than for human use'. It is ironical that, given its origins, Fountains Abbey grew to become the richest Cistercian monastery in England. At the height of its power, it supported 600 lay brothers as well as the priests, and owned huge tracts of land. Flocks of sheep were grazed as far away as Fountains Fell above Malham ★ and the abbey controlled lead mines in Nidderdale. Now all that remains are the skeletons of the beautiful buildings by the river.

The most attractive approach is through the Canal Gates in the tiny village of Studley Roger.

The path goes through the deer park of Studley Hall — the hall itself was burned down in 1946. Here the river has been canalised to form a series of formal lakes which make a delightful setting for the classical statues and the surrounding gardens. It is quite a long walk, and those who do not relish it can more easily reach the abbey itself from the main gate. The great church looks quite magnificent still, with its massive tower in the Perpendicular style, rising high above the roofless nave and transept, where the delicate tracery of the empty windows contrasts with the massive solidity of the pillars. The cloister court, with its superb Norman arches, leads into the cellarium, with its rhythmical pattern of pillars and vaulted ceiling.

Many of the buildings are now no more than outlines of walls on the ground, the stone having been taken away and re-used for other buildings, including the Jacobean Fountains Hall which now houses an exhibition on the abbey. Fountains Abbey and Studley Royal are owned by the National Trust. On **Tour 9**.

Gargrave (103) (SD 9354) 4 miles NW of Skipton
This is a pleasant village on the southern edge of the dales. The dominant feature is the River Aire which cuts through the middle, and everything spreads out and away from the old stone bridge. There is a feeling of spaciousness with broad greens reaching down to the water's edge, though it is not as peaceful as it might be because the busy A65 also runs through the centre.

Fountains Abbey, perhaps the most beautiful of all Britain's monastic remains.

GARSDALE

On the northern edge, the Leeds and Liverpool Canal passes through two locks while the railway passes to the south. On **Tour 2**.

Garsdale (98) (SD 7489) 6 miles E of Sedbergh
Drivers on the A684, between Sedbergh ★ and Garsdale Head ★ could be forgiven for thinking that there is no village in the dale itself. But Garsdale village does exist, a small group of houses centred around a point where the road goes through two right-angled bends to cross the River Clough. The church was rebuilt in 1861, but Easby ★ Abbey had a chaplain here in the thirteenth century. The school was founded in 1634. On a clear day, you can look westward down the valley all the way to Scafell and the peaks of the Lake District.

Danny Bridge once carried the main road through Garsdale over the River Clough.

Garsdale Head (98) (SD 7892) 6 miles W of Hawes
Garsdale Head's main significance is as a station on the Settle and Carlisle Railway, and it is somehow typical of that line that there is scarcely any other building in sight though there was once a branch line down to Hawes ★. Nearby, on the A684, is the equally lonely Moorcock Inn. Garsdale itself stretches all the way down to Sedbergh, with a thin sprinkling of houses but no fewer than six Methodist chapels. On **Tour 4**.

Lonely moorland surrounding the few scattered houses of Garsdale Head village.

Giggleswick village clustered round the tall tower of the fifteenth-century church.

Gayle (98) (SD 8789) ¹/₂ mile S of Hawes
Gayle almost touches Hawes ★ yet can seem a hundred miles away from that busy little town. This ancient village, based on a Viking settlement, is cut by the Duerley Beck which tumbles down between the houses in a series of waterfalls. It is a place of light, narrow streets, while a stone-flagged causeway leads down across the meadows to Hawes church. It is not conventionally pretty, but has a special, austere beauty, its solid stone houses seeming quite at home on the edge of the fells. Industry came here in the eighteenth century, and you can still see the old cotton mill beside the beck. On **Tour 6**.

Giggleswick (98) (SD 8164) adjoining Settle
Giggleswick looks out across the Ribble to the busy market town of Settle ★. The village itself is a delight, with old stone houses grouped around the market cross and a village church that has a handsome fifteenth-century exterior even if the interior turns out to have been given the full, heavy-handed Victorian treatment. Two features dominate the village, one natural and other artificial: the great limestone cliffs of Giggleswick Scar and the public school, founded in 1512, with its copper dome rising high above the chapel.

God's Bridge (92) (NY 9512) 2 miles W of Bowes
This is a natural bridge of rock across the beautiful River Greta. It lies just south of the A66 at the point where the Pennine Way crosses the road.

Gordale Scar see **Malham**

Gouthwaite Reservoir see **Ramsgill**

Grassington (98) (SE 0064)
This large Wharfedale village has become one of the more popular spots with Dales tourists, and visitors are well advised not even to attempt to park in the main square but to go straight to the large car park by the Dales Park Centre on the

The natural rock formation across the Greta, known as God's Bridge.

B6265 Hebden ★ Road.

It is not difficult to see why Grassington is so popular. The main street opens out into a cobbled square, surrounded by a wealth of fine buildings, including Church House with a datestone of 1694, and the Upper Wharfedale Museum. Then the road divides into narrow lanes and a complex of old stone cottages and barns. Near the top of Garrs Lane is Theatre Cottage, converted from a barn that was indeed once used as a theatre, grand enough for the famous Edmund Kean to appear there. Although officially a village, Grassington does boast a Town Hall, originally the Mechanics Institute.

Grassington derives its name from its *Garrs* or enclosures, the small 'Celtic' fields of the early settlers of the sixth and seventh centuries. It owes its obvious prosperity, however, to a later period, when it became the centre of a thriving lead mining industry. The old settlement and the mining remains can be seen on **Walk 3**.

Fortunately for Grassington, the decline in mining coincided with the opening of the branch line from Skipton ★ in 1901, and, although the line was closed by 1930, tourism had become well established. One building that is conspicuously absent is the parish church, for Grassington falls within the parish of Linton ★. One of the attractive walks lies across the fields from the Grassington end of the bridge over the Wharfe

The Upper Wharfedale Museum in Grassington deals with all aspects of life in the dale.

to Linton Falls. These are, in fact, partly artificial, supplying water for the mills on the opposite bank. A footbridge across the river to Linton has been declared unsafe, and is no longer in use.

Grassington is featured on **Tour 2** and **Tour 3** starts there.

Greenhow Hill (99) (SE 1164) 3 miles W of Pateley Bridge
This little village, the highest in Yorkshire at 1300 ft above sea level, shows its origins very clearly. The village pub is the Miners Arms, and the moorland all around is scarred and pockmarked with minings. Lead has been dug here from Roman times to the last century. On **Tours 1** and **3**.

Greta Bridge (92) (NZ 0813) 3 miles SE of Barnard Castle
There is not much to Greta Bridge, but what there is looks remarkably fine. The bridge itself, built in 1773, crosses the Greta near its confluence with the Tees. The coaching inn shows that this was once a main road, but the new A66 passes it by. The gateway once led into Rokeby Park ★, but has also been left isolated by the new road. Down the road by the turn to Wycliffe is Thorpe Farm, a grand building in the Palladian style. That is all, but it is a spot of quiet charm to pause and to wander along the banks of the Greta. **Tour 8** passes this way.

Grinton (98) (SE 0498) 10 miles W of Richmond
This small village by a bridge over the Swale is

49

The church at Grinton is at the end of Corpse Way; its graveyard served the whole valley.

altogether dominated by its church. Its size reflects its importance as the parish church for the whole of the upper dale and the land up to the old Westmoreland border. It was not just the only church, but also the only graveyard, and a track was established down from the fells above Muker ★ , known as the Corpse Way. Journeys from the more distant farms could take two days, the bodies being carried in wickerwork baskets because coffins would have been far too heavy. The inn at Feetham ★ provided a welcome stopping place. The church itself is a fine example of the Perpendicular style, with a twelfth-century font and medieval stained glass.

Grinton was once an important lead mining centre, and the old smelt mill up Cogden Gill to the south is one of the best preserved in the area. The nineteenth-century castellated shooting lodge a little way up the gill is now a youth hostel. Grinton features on **Tours 5** and **6**.

Grisedale (98) (SD 7793) 1 mile NW of Garsdale Head
The hamlet is no more than a scattering of farms, but the little dale itself is a delight. The road simply peters out at its northern end into tracks across Baugh Fell and Wild Boar Fell, so few motorists venture this way. Grisedale is a place for those who appreciate solitude and the simple pleasures of valley and fell. Yet in its time it was quite important, for it was owned by Jervaulx Abbey ★ and the monks established a grange here.

Gunnerside (98) (SD 9598) 15 miles W of Richmond
This little Swaledale village stands at the foot of Gunnerside Gill, along which were some of the most important lead mines in the area. **Tour 6.**

Gunnerside Gill.

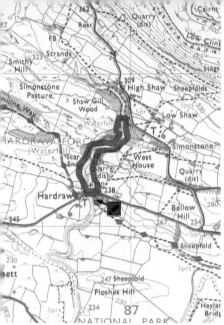

Hardraw Force falls as a single sheet of water, having eroded the rock beneath the lip.

Halton Gill (98) (SD 8876) 8 miles N of Settle
There are few villages in the Dales which can boast such a magnificent setting. The hamlet of Halton Gill sits snugly in the bowl of the hills at the very end of Littondale. The houses are seventeenth century; there is a little school of similar date, but the grandest building is the 'porch' barn, with its huge entrance and prominent porch dated 1829. Halton Gill is a perfect Dales village in miniature. The view back from the hilly road to Stainforth ★ on **Tour 2** is especially memorable.

Crimple viaduct on the Leeds-Harrogate line.

Hardraw (98) (SD 8691) 1 mile N of Hawes
The village itself is tiny, but, by going through the Green Dragon and paying a small fee, you can walk up by the stream to Hardraw Force. The fall cascades over the overhanging lip of a natural rock amphitheatre in a 90-ft high curtain of water. The bottom of the cliff has been eroded away, so that it is possible to walk behind the fall.

Harrogate (104) (SE 3055)
Harrogate has seen great changes in a comparatively short existence. There was virtually no

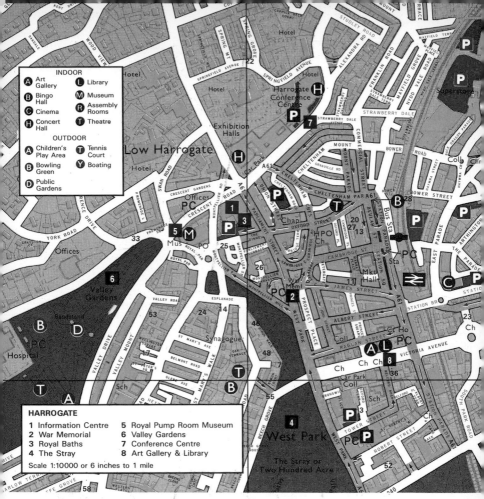

HARROGATE

1 Information Centre
2 War Memorial
3 Royal Baths
4 The Stray
5 Royal Pump Room Museum
6 Valley Gardens
7 Conference Centre
8 Art Gallery & Library

Scale 1:10000 or 6 inches to 1 mile

INDOOR
- A Art Gallery
- B Bingo Hall
- C Cinema
- H Concert Hall
- L Library
- M Museum
- R Assembly Rooms
- T Theatre

OUTDOOR
- A Children's Play Area
- B Bowling Green
- D Public Gardens
- T Tennis Court
- Y Boating

town at all until the growing popularity of spa water at the end of the eighteenth century brought it into prominence. Most of the town centre one sees today was developed in the nineteenth century. Fresh air, of which there is generally an abundance in this hilltop town, combined with the sulphur springs to create the spa. Even the name 'spa' was the invention of a local man, William Slingsby, who noted that the waters were similar to those he had tasted at Spa in Belgium. The original spring that he discovered in 1571 then lay in Knaresborough ★ Forest, and he had the area around it paved. It was named Tewit Well — the word 'tewit' being a local name for the lapwing — and the site is still marked by a little domed building on The Stray (4) near Leeds Road.

The centre of the town, at which many of the elements that give Harrogate its character combine, is the War Memorial (2). It stands surrounded by flower beds and greenery, with streets radiating off in all directions. Parliament Street and Montpellier Parade slope away steeply downhill and, at their junction stands Betty's old-fashioned café, famous for its afternoon teas. Down Parliament Street are shops, many with elaborate iron canopies, and the Royal Baths and Assembly Rooms (3) which together

gave the full spa medical treatment and provided a social centre. Montpellier Parade runs down past a large tract of grassland studded with flower beds. This is part of The Stray (4), in effect a common, which runs all the way round the southern part of the town. It gives a sense of spaciousness, and no building is permitted in the area. When the railway finally reached Harrogate, it had to be sunk down into a deep cutting, so that it slinks into the centre rather shamefacedly. It does, however, reach the edge of town in triumph, sweeping over Crimple Beck on a majestic viaduct that is a major landmark on the approach from Leeds.

Montpellier Parade leads down to an attractive area of antique shops and restaurants, and to the Royal Pump Room Museum (5). The octagonal, domed building of 1842 stands over a sulphur spring and, as well as housing exhibits of local history, it also gives visitors the opportunity to taste the waters. It is to be hoped that the waters improve the health for they do nothing for the taste buds, and the old name 'stinking well' seems all too apt. Across the road is the entrance to the Valley Gardens (6). These are formal gardens with all the trimmings of stream and bandstand, sun pavilion and colonnade. You can walk through the gardens, right out to the heathland of Harlow Car Gardens.

From the Valley Gardens entrance, Crescent Road leads round to the heart of modern Harrogate, the complex of buildings that make up the Conference Centre (7). Some are new and some are old: the Royal Hall, which began as the Kursaal, is used for the celebrated annual music festival as well as housing meetings. The area is surrounded by hotels where, on this occasion, names such as Grand and Majestic seem justified.

Harrogate's other claims to fame are as home to the delectable Farrah's Harrogate toffee and as hosts to the Great Yorkshire show, held in a permanent show ground off Wetherby Road. Start of **Tour 9**.

Montpellier Parade, Harrogate.

Hartlington (98) (SE 0361) 4 miles SE of Grassington

This little hamlet stands across the Wharfe from Burnsall ★ . There is a bridge across the Barben Beck, a former mill and a nineteenth-century hall, but it was once more important and is mentioned in the Domesday Book. On **Tour 1**.

Hawes (98) (SD 8789)

This is one of the most popular centres in the Dales, a market town of wide cobbled streets and little alleyways. The beck that rushes down the hill from Gayle ★ arrives in the centre of the town as a waterfall by the bridge and, in wet weather, becomes a spectacular torrent. Although Hawes is not an ancient market town — it did not receive its charter until the beginning of the eighteenth century — it is a thriving one and, on market days, the town is packed with people. The Auction Mart is the most important livestock sale in the district. It was in Hawes in 1897 that a factory was established to make the famous Wensleydale cheese, and it is still made in the town. Another traditional craft practised in the town is ropemaking, which visitors can watch at W R Outhwaite & Son, whose methods of working are much as they were when the firm began in 1905.

The railway that ran down Wensleydale was closed in 1959 and the old station buildings are now home to the Upper Dales Folk Museum and Park Information Centre. Hawes is the starting point for **Tour 5** and **Tour 4** passes through the town.

Hawes sits in a hollow by the River Ure. It is an ancient market town and has become a popular tourist centre. The railway down Wensleydale is closed but the station houses the Upper Dales Folk Museum (above).

Hebden (98) (SE 0263) 2 miles E of Grassington
The village stretches along the bank of the
Hebden Brook as it makes its way down to the
Wharfe. The narrow gorge of the beck is unusual for this area in showing dark gritstone rock
instead of the more familiar limestone. There
are attractive walks both upstream to the moors
and downstream to the grassy banks of the
Wharfe, and these walks form a part of **Walk 3**
and the village features on **Tour 3**.

Hellifield (103) (SD 8556) 3 miles SE of Settle
Hellifield became important in the nineteenth
century, boasting two stations — one on the line
south to Blackburn, now used only by freight,
and the other on the line from Skipton ★. Today
it is well known to railway enthusiasts taking
excursions on the Settle ★ and Carlisle line
which turns off to the north at Settle Junction. It
developed to become an important cattle market.
    To the south of the town in Hellifield Park are
the ruined remains of a peel tower. This was a
fortified house of 1441, with towers at each
corner of a walled square as protection from
raiders coming down from the north. It was
partly demolished in 1954.

Horsehouse (98) (SE 0481) 8 miles NE of Kettlewell
A little Coverdale village of considerable charm
with a terrace of stone cottages looking across at
the Thwaite Arms. In the days of the pack
horses, which gave the village its name, there
were three inns in the village. To balance the
inns there was the chapel and the little church, a
chapel of ease. On **Tour 3**.

Horton in Ribblesdale (98) (SD 8072) 5 miles N of
Settle
Horton is one of the great potholing centres of
the region, most of the caves being clustered
round the lower slopes of Pen-y-ghent, the
shapely hill that dominates the view to the east.

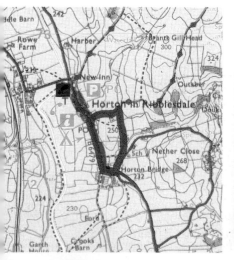

The village itself sits under rows of natural limestone scars, and the even greater scars made by
the still active quarries. The quarries may not be
especially lovely, but they are undeniably impressive. Surprisingly perhaps, Horton managed to retain much of its charm, for the old part
of the village clustered round the church belongs much more to the older world of farming
than to the new of the quarries. It is a good
centre for walking as well as potholing — the
Pennine Way passes through — and there are
pleasant strolls by the river or more energetic
walks on the slopes of the moor.

Hubberholme (98) (SD 9278) 4 miles N of Kettlewell
This is a small hamlet, but full of interest and
blessed by a most beautiful setting. The river
splashes and gurgles under the bridge that divides the two prominent buildings, the church
and the village inn. The church is a rare delight
with an elaborately carved rood loft and screen,
and modern pews by Robert Thompson, who
has left his distinctive signature, a little carved
mouse, on each of them. The George Inn is old
and homely and it is here each New Year's Day
that the Hubberholme Parliament meets to
auction off the tenancy of a field, the proceeds
going to charity. The wooded valley is as delightful a setting as one could hope for. **Walk 10**
and **Tour 6** explore the surrounding countryside.

*The rood loft and screen in the Church of St
Michael, Hubberholme.*

Elizabethan manor house, now home to the local museum.

Tour 10 has a suggested stroll on the moors, where the Cow and Calf rocks are a prominent feature. There was once a Bull rock, but it was quarried away and the stone was used in local buildings.

Ingleton (98) (SD 6972) 4 miles SE of Kirkby Lonsdale
Ingleton sits at the meeting point of three rivers, where the Twiss and the Doe combine forces to create the Greta. It might have been just another pleasant Dales market town if the arrival of the railways in 1849 had not opened it up for tourism. Its situation is immediately appealing, crouched down under the shadow of Ingleborough, but it was the watery connection that seemed to offer the greatest attraction. The locals banded together to form an 'Improve-

Hunters Stone (98) (SD 9976) 4½ miles NE of Kettlewell
A minor road leads from Coverham ★ through Coverdale and across the lonely hills to Kettlewell ★. At the very top of the dale, just before the road starts its steep descent to Kettlewell, stands a single stone inscribed with a cross. It was set there as a marker centuries ago by the monks of Coverham Abbey. On **Tour 3**.

Ilkley (104) (SE 1247)
This Wharfedale town is less well known than the moorland to the south where, as all good Yorkshiremen know, it is fatal to go without a hat. It enjoyed a brief popularity as a spa, but it remains a small, pleasant, and unassuming place. It does have a long history, which only really appears in the church. The Romans had a fort here, parts of which can be seen in the churchyard, and two Roman altars are built into the church tower. The Viking age is recalled in three Runic crosses. Behind the church is a restored

Left: *The tower of Ingleton church is Perpendicular, but the rest mainly Victorian.*
Above: *The pack-horse bridge across the Swale at Ivelet. Note the typical steep arch.*

ment Association' to open up the wooded valleys with their spectacular waterfalls. The results of their efforts can still be enjoyed in the 'Falls Walk', which explores the valleys of the Twiss and the Ure, an incomparable mixture of wooded gorges and sparkling falls. There is a charge for the 4-mile walk, but the cost is more than amply repaid. Two miles outside Ingleton, beside the B6255 are the White Scar show caves. Both town and caves feature on **Tour 4**.

Ivelet (98) (SD 9398) 1 mile W of Gunnerside
The hamlet on the northern bank of the Swale is mainly notable for its quite extraordinary fine pack-horse bridge over the river. It has one single, high, graceful arch. It is suggested as worth a short detour from **Tour 6**.

Jervaulx Abbey (99) (SE 1785) 4 miles SE of Leyburn
The name represents the Norman spelling for

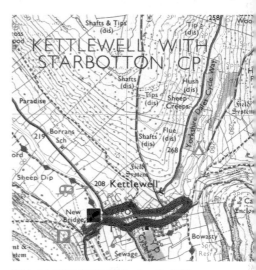

The remains of twelfth-century Jervaulx Abbey — home of Wensleydale cheese.

Ure Vale. It is said that this Cistercian abbey was founded here in 1156 when a party of monks lost their way, but saw a vision of the Virgin Mary at this spot. The last abbot was a whole-hearted opponent of Henry VIII at the time of the Dissolution — and was hanged at Tyburn for his efforts. As a result, the abbey suffered far greater damage than other great institutions such as Fountains ★ or Bolton ★. Nevertheless it is still a lovely and atmospheric site, and the abbey has one non-religious claim to fame: the monks here were the first to make Wensleydale cheese. The handsome Jervaulx Hall next to the site was built from abbey stone. **Tour 3** goes past the abbey.

Keld (92) (NY 8901) 6 miles N of Hawes
Keld is a quiet, tucked-away hamlet, lying just off the B6270. It has many of the attractions of other similar dales villages — a tight cluster of old stone houses, a chapel, the youth hostel, and, rather more surprisingly, a Literary Institute. Keld's main appeal, however, lies with its Swaledale setting. Here the river plunges into a limestone gorge, reminiscent of famous Dovedale in Derbyshire, and its waters are swelled by the Kisdon Force waterfall. **Tour 5** comes to Keld and the river valley is explored on **Walk 8**.

Kettlewell (98) (SD 9772) 6 miles N of Grassington
Kettlewell has a good deal in common with Grassington ★. Both are Wharfedale villages, both well-established market towns which grew in prosperity with lead mining, and both are now popular tourist centres from which to explore the river valley and the surrounding fells. Of the two, however, Kettlewell is generally the more peaceful, and is a pleasant place to linger, encouraged perhaps by the presence of three old inns. The church is largely Victorian, but represents the plain and simple style rather than the usual gloomy Gothic; it has stained-glass windows from the William Morris studios. This is a recommended stopping place on **Tour 3**.

Kildwick (104) (SE 0146) 4 miles S of Skipton
This little Airedale village stands astride the Leeds and Liverpool Canal, and a short walk down the towpath gives you the sturdy essence of the place, with dark stone buildings rising sheer from the water. It has a surprisingly large and impressive church with box pews and a somewhat dour Jacobean Hall, now a restaurant.

Kilnsey (98) (SD 9767) 3 miles N of Grassington
The one building of note is the inn and that, like the rest of the village, is literally overshadowed by Kilnsey Crag. The great limestone cliff rises above the B6160 to be topped by a dark, frowning overhang. It ranks with Malham Cove ★ as the most dramatic cliff in the region. There are few traces now of the Monastic Grange from which the Fountains Abbey ★ estates were administered. On **Tour 2**.

Mastiles Gate across Kilnsey Moor was used by the monks of Fountains Abbey as a road.

KIRKBY LONSDALE

Kirkby Lonsdale (97) (SD 6178)

Situated in the south-east corner of Cumbria, Kirkby Lonsdale stands on a high bank overlooking the River Lune. The town seems to represent a halfway point between the limestone of the Pennines and the granite of the Lake District. Its solid eighteenth-century houses and cobbled streets make it a pleasure to explore. It has been the market town for the Lune valley since as early as the thirteenth century, and is almost completely unspoiled.

The Information Centre (1) is in Main Street, south of the Market Square (3). The square was built in 1822 and contains the only ugly thing in the town, a covered market cross which doubles as a bus shelter. Before the square was built, markets were held in the streets around the church: Fairbank, Horsemarket, Swinemarket, and Market Street.

To the north, St Mary's church (8) dates from the twelfth century and probably stands on the site of a Saxon church which was given to York Abbey in 1093 by Ivo de Tailbois 'for the good of his soul, and that of Lucy his Wife'. The abbey seems to have responded by building a new church. The west end has a fine Norman archway beneath the tower and inside there are three Norman ribbed arches.

Follow the footpath to the north of the church to the Gazebo, and then walk along the Brow to Ruskin's View (7), marked by a plaque in the wall. He considered it '...one of the loveliest scenes in England, therefore in the world. Whatever moorland hill, and sweet river, and English forest foliage can be at their best is gathered here...'.

Returning to the churchyard, the Radical Steps (6) lead down to the river. At the bottom there is a footpath running south along the river bank to the Devil's Bridge (2). The bridge has three graceful arches and used to carry the old turnpike road from Kendal to Keighley; its age is uncertain. Some 200 yards further downstream is the Devil's Neck Collar, a circular hole in a large block of limestone that sticks out into the river.

To return from the Gazebo to the centre of town, take the left-hand path through the churchyard and walk through a narrow alleyway into the cobbled Swinemarket. The old market cross (5) stands in front of Abbot's Hall: it was moved here in 1819 from Market Street because of the traffic. Mill Brow (4), which runs steeply down to the river, once had seven waterwheels powered by a stream which is now channelled underground. The mills made snuff, calico, and horse-blankets.

Kirkby Lonsdale is the starting point for **Tour 4**, and the riverside walk from Devil's Bridge is recommended for a short stroll.

Kirkby Malham (98) (SD 8961) 1 mile S of Malham

The village is, as the name suggests, a settlement which, unlike Malham ★, has a church. It

KIRKBY LONSDALE

1 Information Centre
2 Devil's Bridge
3 Market Square
4 Mill Brow
5 Market Cross
6 Radical Steps
7 Ruskin's View
8 St Mary's

Scale 1:10000 or 6 inches to 1 mile

A fine terrace of solid, seventeenth-century stone cottages at Kirkby Malham.

is every bit as attractive as its more famous neighbour. The church is a fine example of Perpendicular architecture, which curiously fell under the jurisdiction of the abbey at West Dereham in Norfolk. The abbey appointed the vicars, and it would be interesting to know what a clergyman from the flat lands of East Anglia made of this region of hills and crags. The church register records a wedding where Oliver Cromwell signed as a witness. Kirkby Malham is on **Tour 2**.

Kirkby Stephen (91) (NY 7708) 9 miles SE of Appleby

The Cumbrian market town of Kirkby Stephen stands near the head of the lovely, and much undervalued, valley of the River Eden. At its heart is the market square, with a ring of cobbles marking out the old bull-baiting area. Between

The church or kirk of Kirkby Stephen that gave the town its name rises above the houses and shops at the edge of the market place.

the church and the square stand the pedimented colonnade of the cloisters, designed in 1810 as a screen to separate the bustle of the market from the peace of the church. The impressive sandstone church with its tall tower is flanked by the old parsonage of 1677 and the grammar school, founded in 1566 and now a comprehensive. The town also boasts a knitting gallery near the market square where, in the eighteenth-century, the knitters sat producing stockings for the army and navy. Kirkby Stephen is on **Tour 7**.

Knaresborough (104) (SE 3557) 3 miles E of Harrogate

Knaresborough is a delightful old market town in a dramatic setting, high above the River Nidd. At its heart was the castle which stands on the edge of a tall sandstone cliff, and it was under its protection that the town grew and prospered. Today the centre of the town's life is the Market Place (**1**), still in use and still retaining some, at least, of its original character. The market cross still stands, surrounded by cobbles and, among the shops, is one that claims to be the oldest chemist's shop in England; if appearances are anything to go by, then the claim would seem to be well and truly justified.

From the corner of the Market Place, Kirkgate leads away steeply downhill towards the railway and the church. This is an area full of character, the street lined with old stone buildings. Then the way divides, the high-level route leading to the church, while another street leads even more steeply down to the riverside. This is Water Bag Bank, a reminder of the days when donkeys used to struggle up the hill carrying bags full of river water as the town's sole source of water. At the bottom is an attractive thatched cottage, and a much larger house decorated in a black-and-white chequered pattern. This, although much altered over the years, was origi-

KNARESBOROUGH

nally the lodge where King John stayed when hunting in the Forest of Knaresborough. Recent research has revealed a new connection between the king and the town. A set of royal accounts shows that he paid £4.13.9d (£4.70) and 9s.4d (47p) to feed 1,000 poor people in 1210. This was Maundy Money and Knaresborough now claims to have taken over from Rochester as the site of the very first Maundy distribution.

The river itself is pleasant and there are boats to be hired, but its most famous feature is the railway viaduct (2) which took its decorative theme from the nearby castle, and comes complete with battlements, turrets, and arrow slits. Beyond it is one of the two road bridges across the Nidd, High Bridge — nowhere near as spectacular as its railway neighbour. Across the main road is the entrance to Conyngham Hall (3) where grounds have been developed as a public park. At the town end of the bridge is the curiously named World's End pub — and to get an explanation of the name you need to cross the bridge to Long Walk which follows the river back all the way to Low Bridge. Just over halfway along is Mother Shipton's Cave (4). Ursula Shipton was a fifteenth-century prophet, whose slightly cryptic verses foretold the arrival of iron

ships, aeroplanes, and other modern inventions — and also foretold the end of the world, hence the pub name. A little beyond the cave is the Dropping Well (5). Water dribbles slowly across a limestone face, and anything hung below the stony curtain gradually becomes petrified. Stony teddy bears hang beside solidified gloves and socks. Apart from these attractions, the walk provides a pleasant woodland stroll with fine views of the town.

At Low Bridge, cross the road and walk a little way up to the right. Opposite the Mother Shipton Inn is a cliff face with two curious buildings, carved from the rock (6). The first is a rare example of a wayside shrine, the chapel of Our Lady of the Crag, which was built under a licence from Henry IV. The second is, if anything, even more remarkable, Fort Montagu, a grand name for a four-storey house carved out of the rock by a local weaver. Energetic visitors can climb the steps up the cliff face.

The most interesting route back to the town centre is by the river or Waterside. There, under the shadow of the high sandstone cliffs, is a last reminder of the industrial past of the town. The old mill (7) was built in 1791 to spin cotton, but was soon converted to making linen, and worked on right up to 1972. Just beyond the mill, the

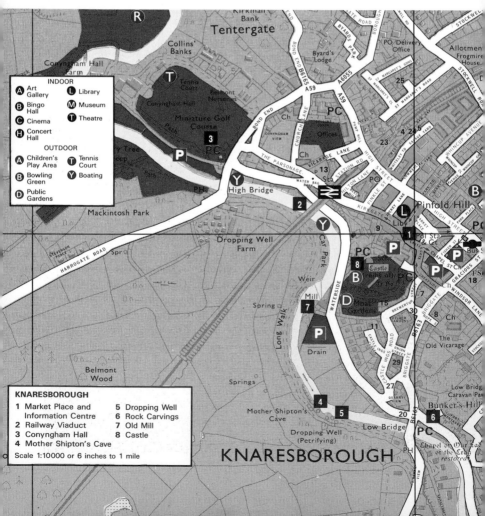

KNARESBOROUGH

1 Market Place and Information Centre
2 Railway Viaduct
3 Conyngham Hall
4 Mother Shipton's Cave
5 Dropping Well
6 Rock Carvings
7 Old Mill
8 Castle

Scale 1:10000 or 6 inches to 1 mile

Tiny Langthwaite is, in fact, the largest village in Arkengarthdale.

gardens have been constructed in terraces and a steep, winding path leads up to the remains of the castle (**8**). Its precise origins are unknown, but it is believed to have been built by John of Gaunt. It was here that the knights fled after they murdered Thomas à Becket. It was held by the Royalists during the Civil War and consequently suffered the inevitable fate of being pulled down by Cromwell. The keep still stands, and the old court house, which houses a local history museum with exhibits including the surveying instruments of the remarkable eighteenth-century road builder, Blind Jack Metcalf. The Castle keep itself provides a last and spectacular view of the town and its river. **Tour 9.**

Langcliffe (98) (SD 8265) 1 mile N of Settle
This is a pleasant little village, overlooked by the crags of Langcliffe Scar. There is a number of large caves in the scar, notably Victoria and Attermire. These are among the oldest caves in the area which are known to have been inhabited, and carved antler tools have been found dating back more than 10,000 years. Bones also provide evidence of animals that once lived here. The mammoth is perhaps not too surprising an inhabitant from the Ice Age, but it seems decidedly odd to think of the Yorkshire Dales as once being warm enough to provide a home to hippopotamus and rhinoceros.

Leyburn's market place ringed by handsome Georgian and early Victorian buildings.

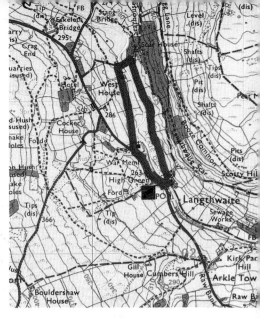

Langthwaite (92) (NZ 0002) 8 miles S of Barnard Castle
Langthwaite is the nearest thing to a village in the whole of Arkengarthdale. There is a compact muddle of houses and a single street leading to Booze — which has no pub! There is little of note in the village itself, apart from a rather stylish early nineteenth-century church, but the setting of high fells scarred by lead mine workings is superb. Suggested as a stroll around the village. On **Tour 5.**

Leighton (99) (SE 1679) 4 miles W of Masham
The reservoir is a favourite spot for birdwatchers, particularly in winter when it is an important refuge for wildfowl, including a large population of goosanders. In the woods to the east is the 'Druid's Temple', a miniature Stonehenge which is, in fact, a nineteenth-century folly. On **Tour 3.**

Leyburn (99) (SE 1190)
Leyburn stands at a junction of four main roads which make it a natural choice as a market town,

though it did not receive a charter until the seventeenth century. It has an air of genial prosperity, with a number of solidly handsome eighteenth- and nineteenth-century houses. To the west of the town is the long natural terrace, overlooking the River Ure, known as The Shawl, where Mary Queen of Scots was recaptured after escaping imprisonment in Bolton Castle ★. Start of **Tour 6.**

Linton (98) (SD 9962) 1 mile S of Grassington
A monument on the green commemorates Linton's success in the Prettiest Village in the North competition of 1949, and nothing has happened since to spoil that beauty. The stream through the village green is crossed by an old clapper bridge and a high-arched pack-horse bridge. The surrounding stone houses are old and dignified and the Fountaine Inn looks cheerily inviting. The post office is housed in a building of 1679 and the Old Hall is now a youth hostel. The one surprising note is struck by the Fountaine Hospital, built in 1721 as almshouses for six poor men or women. For such a modest purpose in such a small village, it has a remarkably formal, classical style and has been attributed to Vanbrugh.

The church, close by the river, also serves the population of neighbouring Grassington ★. It is as delightful as everything else here, its outside graced by an odd little corbelled belfry, while the inside has a Norman arcade and sumptuous roof bosses. The footbridge to Grassington ★ has been declared unsafe and closed.

Litton (98) (SD 9074) 2 miles NW of Arncliffe
Although it gives beautiful Littondale its name, Litton itself is a tiny, peaceful spot with no

The gentle hills of Upper Nidderdale near Lofthouse.

obvious signs of importance. A few houses, a church, a pub, and a couple of bridges, but in such a setting one would be greedy to ask for more. Litton is on **Tour 2.**

Lofthouse (99) (SE 1073) 6 miles NW of Pateley Bridge
This Nidderdale village sits near the end of the long narrow valley, is a typical small cluster of old stone houses, but has a few surprises up its sleeve. The drinking trough has rhymes carved in the side, such as this:
If you want to be healthy, wealthy and stout Use plenty of cold water inside and out.
And, if the antique shop looks to be an odd shape, this is because it started off as the station for the Nidd Valley Light Railway which began its brief career in 1906. But Lofthouse's main claim to fame lies just to the west of the village — How Stean, a dramatic gorge cut deep into the rock through which the Stean Gill rushes. Directions for reaching the gorge, which can be visited on paying an entrance charge, are given on **Walk 4** which starts at Lofthouse. The village is on **Tour 3.**

Long Preston (103) (SD 8358) 4 miles S of Settle
Long Preston is as long and straggling as its name suggests, with remains of the old Roman fort by the church. It is best known for 'Long Preston Peggy' who, according to folk song, walked over the moor to see Bonnie Prince Charlie and, somewhat absent-mindedly it seems, captured Manchester for the Jacobites while she was there. It is on **Tour 2.**

The unique and extraordinary limestone pavement above Malham Cove.

Airedale, close to the most dramatic sights in the whole of the Dales, Malham Cove and Gordale Scar, both of which can be visited as described in **Walk 2**.

Malham Cove is a natural amphitheatre, formed by a sheer limestone cliff topped by a limestone pavement. Gordale Scar is a deep, tortuous cleft in the rocks down which the stream cascades in a series of waterfalls. Another large waterfall, Janet's Foss, can be seen near the bottom.

The limestone cliffs at Malham Cove are among the most spectacular sights in the Dales. Once a waterfall gushed down the face.

Malham (98) (SD 9063) 5 miles E of Settle
Malham is one of the most popular villages in the Dales. It is certainly a delightful spot with a busy stream running through the green, a cluster of old houses, two inns, and a youth hostel. But its popularity lies in its setting rather than in the village itself. It sits at the very head of

63

MARKET BROUGH

Also nearby is Malham Tarn, a wide, lonely expanse owned by the National Trust. The Field Studies Council run educational courses from Tarn House. The stream from the southern end of the tarn vanishes into sink holes in the limestone to re-emerge at the foot of Malham Cove. You can stroll to the tarn from the small car park by the Malham-to-Arncliffe ★ road.

Malham is on **Tour 2**. and there is ample parking space by the National Park Centre.

Market Brough see **Brough**

Marrick (99) (SE 0798) 6 miles SW of Richmond
Marrick is best known for its priory, the remains of which can be reached by a walk through the woods to the south and then down to the river on the flight of steps known as the 'Nun's Causey'. Originally, there were 365 of them, but many are broken or missing, and those who fancy an easier and less hazardous approach can take the path down from the road near Fremington, to the west of Marrick. The former Benedictine priory has a new building set inside the shell, which functions as a sort of spiritual youth hostel.

Marske (92) (SZ 1000) 4 miles W of Richmond
This pretty little Swaledale village is surrounded by woodland, and the busy Marske beck runs through the centre under a fifteenth-century bridge. The church has unusual painted box pews and Marske Hall adds its own note of dignity to the hamlet.

Masham (99) (SE 2280) 8 miles NW of Ripon
This very attractive little market town is well worth a pause for exploration.

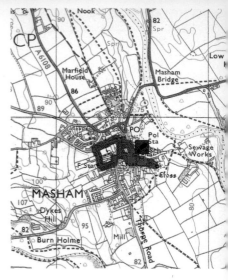

Coming into the town on the main road, one of the first buildings to catch the eye by the bridge over the Ure is a large malting — a clue to one reason why many people stop here! The heart of the town is its market square and market cross. At the corner of the square is the very grand church which has grown and developed through the centuries. The earliest relic is the carved shaft of a Saxon cross. The Norman tower is topped by a fifteenth-century octagonal lantern and, above that, is a tall spire. Inside there is a fine carved stone pillar, a quite splendid marble monument showing Sir Marmaduke and Lady Wyvell, each leaning nonchalantly on

Theakston's Brewery at Masham. The Black Bull in Paradise has presumably been guaranteed endless supplies of Old Peculier.

Racehorses returning from a training run on Middleham Low Moor.

an elbow, and there is a good twentieth-century window with an ambivalent attitude to wildlife — on one side St George kills a dragon and on the other St Francis feeds the birds.

Masham's fame among the beer-drinking fraternity rests with the Theakston Brewery, home of the notorious strong beer, Old Peculier. There is a visitor centre, telling the story of the brewery since its foundation in 1827. After that one can go, appropriately, to see glass being made at Uredale Glass in the Market Place.

Middleham (99) (SE 1287) 2 miles S of Leyburn
There has been a castle at Middleham since the Norman Conquest. The original motte-and-bailey earthworks can be seen to the south of the town. The succeeding castle, whose ruins dominate the town, has a massive twelfth-century tower, surrounded by high walls and a dry moat. The castle was held by the Neville family from the thirteenth century, and it became the favourite home of Richard III. After the Battle of Bosworth Field, the castle went into decline, and eventual ruin. It is open to visitors. Middleham's other claim to fame is as a training centre for race-horses, which exercise on Middleham Moor.

Middlesmoor (99) (SE 0974) 7 miles NW of Pateley Bridge
This tight-knit little village of stone houses, joined by a maze of cobbled streets, is a delight. It sits perched up on a high hilltop and, from the churchyard, there is a superb view right down Nidderdale. It is visited on **Walk 4**.

Muker (98) (SD 9097) 5 miles N of Hawes
This attractive little village sits perched on a ledge above the Straw beck, close to its confluence with the Swale. The setting is idyllic and the little Farmer's Arms is everything a country inn should be, and makes an ideal place to pause for refreshment on **Walk 8**.

Nateby (91) (NY 7706) 1 mile S of Kirkby Stephen
This little village has an attractive setting in the Eden Valley. It boasts one quite magnificent building, fourteenth-century Wharton Hall, which is still occupied and lies across the river to the south. The description of how to reach it is given in **Walk 11**. Nateby is on **Tour 7**.

Newbiggin (98) (SD 9985) 2 miles S of Aysgarth
Newbiggin lies in the very lush, green valley of Bishopdale, a typical linear village of farmsteads that peters out into a track. Further up the dale to the west, 2 miles beyond the Newbiggin turn off the B6160, is West New House, a splendid example of an early seventeenth-century Pennine long house, in which the house, with the mullioned windows, and the barn form a continuous unit under the one roof. West New House is on **Tour 6**.

Newbiggin-on-Lune (91) (NY 7005) 5 miles SW of Kirkby Stephen
The village which is, paradoxically, nearly a mile from the Lune, has now been bypassed by the A685, leaving it as a pleasantly peaceful backwater. Houses stand round a small green, and the late Victorian church makes an attractive focal point. On **Tour 7**.

Newby Hall (99) (SE 3467) 3 miles SE of Ripon
This late seventeenth-century house owes most of its present appearance to Robert Adam. It houses a fine collection of classical sculpture and Gobelin tapestries. The park and gardens are particularly fine, extending down to the River Ure. There is also an excellent miniature passenger-carrying steam railway. Newby Hall is on **Tour 9**.

North Stainmore (92) (NY 8315) 2 miles E of Brough
The name is derived from Stoney Moor and seems altogether apt. This is a lonely spot on a lonely road, with a few houses, the Punch Bowl, once a coaching inn, and a Victorian church, now redundant. But the situation is magnificent with wide views of the surrounding country — which is why the Romans established the signal station, the scant remains of which can be seen on the knoll to the south of the main road.

Otley (104) (SE 2045) 4 miles E of Ilkley

Otley could easily have been absorbed into either Leeds or Bradford if a line of gritstone crags, the Chevin, had not got in the way. As it is, Otley remains proudly independent. The town's history goes back a very long way: the Manor was granted to the Archbishopric of York in the tenth century and the market charter was given by Henry III in 1222. The market, with its Butter Cross, is still at the heart of the town, but its character changed with the Industrial Revolution when woollen mills arrived. It also became an important centre for manufacturing printing machines. Otley has one very famous son — Chippendale the furniture maker was born here.

The original church of Otley was founded in the seventh century though all that is left of that age are fragments of crosses. The churchyard does, however, have a strange memorial, designed as a tunnel, complete with portals. It commemorates the thirty men who died building nearby Bramhope tunnel on the Leeds and Thirsk Railway.

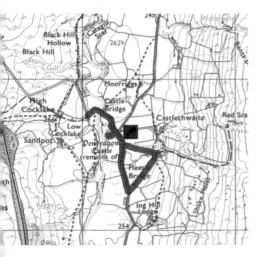

The former flax mill at Pateley Bridge.

Oughtershaw (98) (SD 8781) 5 miles S of Hawes

A pretty little hamlet tucked away in a narrow, lonely valley that runs down to Langstrothdale. The Oughtershaw Beck on which it stands will go on to broaden and deepen, and change its name to the River Wharfe. On **Tour 6**.

Parcevall Hall see **Skyreholme**

Pateley Bridge (99) (SE 1565)

The town has grown up around the main street that climbs steeply from the bridge over the Nidd. This is millstone grit country, and the dark stone could have made the town seem somewhat gloomy if the locals had not liberally bedecked it with flowers. It is an interesting town of contrasts: the houses and shops on the main street show a classical elegance and simplicity, but between are little alleyways leading to secretive, secluded courtyards. The Nidderdale Museum is housed in the Victorian workhouse, which was once home to the navvies who worked on the Nidderdale reservoirs — and there is a good deal of fascinating material on their work in the museum.

Pateley Bridge has traditionally had a dual role: as a market for the hill farmers and as an industrial centre, based on lead mining and textiles. A survivor from the textile world is the old Foster Beck Flax Mill, with its great waterwheel reaching the full height of the building. It stands beside the road up Nidderdale to Ramsgill ★ and is now the Watermill Inn. Pateley Bridge is the starting point for **Tour 1**.

Pendragon Castle (91) (NY 7802) 4 miles S of Kirkby Stephen

A romantic ruin which, sadly perhaps, has little or no connection with Uther Pendragon, father of King Arthur. The fortress is Norman, designed to protect the local farmers from the

Pendragon Castle by the River Eden.

The impressive Yorke Arms (above) stands beside the large village green at Ramsgill. The nearby Gouthwaite reservoir (below) on the River Nidd is famous for its bird life.

Border raiders coming down from Scotland. It was not entirely successful for it was burned by the Scots in 1341 and again in 1541. It was restored by the indefatigable Lady Anne Clifford but, at her death, was again allowed to fall into ruin. It stands beside the B6259 and is a recommended stopping place for a stroll round the ruins and down to the River Eden on **Tour 7**.

Plumpton Rocks (104) (SE 3553) 2 miles E of Harrogate
This is a popular beauty spot beside the Wetherby road where huge gritstone blocks tower up above a wooded lake. The site is on **Tour 9**.

Ramsgill (99) (SE 1171) 4 miles NW of Pateley Bridge
This is a small Nidderdale village, with a large green and a surprisingly grand hotel, The Yorke Arms. It is a good place to stop for a stroll along the footpath that crosses the top of Gouthwaite Reservoir ★ , a favourite place for birdwatchers, and over 200 species have been recorded. The village's other claim to fame is as birthplace of the notorious murderer, Eugene Aram. Ramsgill is on **Tour 3**.

Ravenstonedale (91) (NY 7204) 4 miles SW of Kirkby Stephen
This most attractive Cumbrian village, now bypassed by the A685, is centred on a long main street that climbs steeply up beside the Scandal Beck. Its principal feature is the church, which seems packed with unusual features. Outside is a sundial of 1700. Inside, the box pews, instead of facing the altar, face each other across the aisle. The splendid three-decker pulpit has a special seat for the parson's wife, and there is a window to Elizabeth Gaunt, sentenced by Judge Jefferies to be burned at Tyburn. Ravenstonedale is on **Tour 7**.

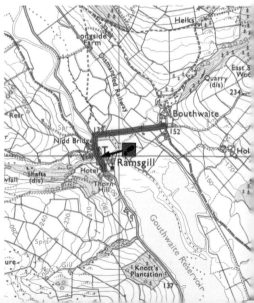

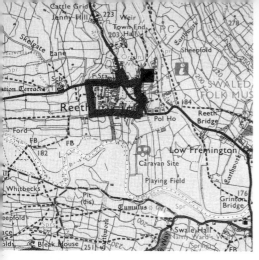

Looking down on the village of Reeth, centred on the large green. Beyond, the hills end at Fremington Edge above Arkengarthdale.

Redmire (98) (SE 0491) 5 miles W of Leyburn
This is a charming village of old stone houses surrounding a green on which stands an ancient and massive oak tree. The village post office has an interesting history, having been used as a drill hall for volunteers for the Napoleonic Wars. The church, with some of its old Norman features still intact, lies ½ mile away to the southeast, while, to the south, is the River Ure and the Redmire force. **Walk 9** passes through Redmire.

Reeth (98) (SE 0399) 12 miles W of Richmond
The attraction of Reeth lies as much in its situ-

ation as in its own intrinsic merits. It has a wonderfully airy location on a plateau above the Swale with wide views round to the surrounding hills. Everything about Reeth gives it a feeling of spaciousness for, at its heart, is a wide green and the old cobbled market area. In its day it has been a centre for lead mining and knitting, a centre for the farming community, and it is now a popular tourist centre. A small museum is devoted to local history. This is a recommended spot for a stroll on **Tour 5**.

Ribblehead see **Chapel-le-Dale**

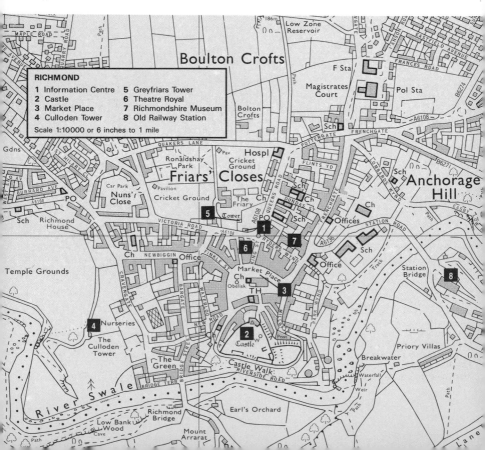

RICHMOND

1 Information Centre	5 Greyfriars Tower
2 Castle	6 Theatre Royal
3 Market Place	7 Richmondshire Museum
4 Culloden Tower	8 Old Railway Station

Scale 1:10000 or 6 inches to 1 mile

Richmond (92) (NZ 1701)

Richmond provides a feast for admirers of good architecture, and especially for those whose tastes favour the eighteenth century. Yet its origins and its overall plan developed eight centuries earlier, in the years following the Norman Conquest. Alan Rufus began building a fortress on the promontory above the Swale in 1071 and, by the twelfth century, the massive keep — standing 100 feet high, its walls 11 feet thick — was completed. There were further additions over the years, but it is the keep that still dominates both castle and town.

The castle (2) is the obvious starting point for any tour. From its walls one can look down on the Market Place (3) which fans out below it. It seems very likely that, once, this area fell within the outer bailey, protected by the castle walls. The other essential unifying feature of Richmond also becomes plain — the use of stone for building and pantiles which give a rich, rippling colour to the roofs of the town. The Market Place itself has a distinctive Georgian look to it: the town hall dates from that period, an obelisk has replaced the market cross, and the King's Head Hotel looks grandly imposing. In the centre of the square is the twelfth-century chapel of the Holy Trinity, which has served many functions over the years and is now the Regimental Museum of the Green Howards.

From the Market Place, New Road — 'new' in the eighteenth century — leads down to the town bridge, another eighteenth-century addition. Before the bridge is reached you come to The Bar, a narrow street which does contain a 'bar', one of the old gateways and all that re-

The great keep of Richmond Castle dominates this view of the town.

mains of the town walls. The steep streets leading down to the river, including cobbled Bridge Street, contain a rich variety of fine Georgian houses. Just above the bridge is The Green from which one can look out to a splendidly ornate Georgian folly, the Culloden Tower. (4) Turning back up the hill you come out at Newbiggin, one of the medieval thoroughfares, but now once again showing an urbane eighteenth-century face to the world. From here you pass back into the area of the walled town via Finkle Street and Friars Wynd. The latter name does not mislead. There was a Franciscan Friary here, but all that remains now is the tall fifteenth-century tower, the Greyfriars tower (5).

One of Richmond's real gems can be seen in Victoria Road. The Theatre Royal (6) scarcely warrants a second glance from the outside, but inside is a beautifully preserved little Georgian theatre. It was built in 1788 by Samuel Butler, a well-known actor-manager of the day, and it is all as it was then — even down to the colour scheme. It is a unique survivor, and visitors can see the small theatre museum and go on a conducted tour of the whole building. The best way of all to see the theatre, however, is by going to a performance, for the theatre is still very much in use. There is a local history museum in Ryder's Wynd (7), and one other building deserves special mention. Richmond had a particularly fine railway station and, when the line closed, it was most imaginatively converted into a garden centre (8). On **Tour 8**.

Ripley Castle has lost its war-like appearance after being rebuilt in the eighteenth century.

Ripley (99) (SE 2860) 3 miles N of Harrogate, off A61

The village is very much centred on the castle, which has been home to the Ingilby family since the fourteenth century. The present house, which is open to the public, was rebuilt in 1780 and the grounds were landscaped by Capability Brown. The church is mostly fourteenth century and has a strange medieval 'weeping cross' in the churchyard, with eight niches where penitents could kneel. Rather more sinister are the pockmarks left by Roundhead bullets, and marks on the east wall of the church where Royalist prisoners were lined up and shot. The village itself is a planned estate village, modelled to the ideas of Sir William Amcotts Ingilby who based it on a village in Alsace Lorraine. It has a typical French Hôtel de Ville, or village hall, though the Gothic terraces are more English in style. The village is featured on **Tour 9.**

Ripon (99) (SE 3171) 10 miles N of Harrogate

At first sight, Ripon may seem to be no more than a large market town, but its cathedral gives it the status of a city, and the citizens are quite rightly proud of the fact and careful guardians of their ancient traditions. The settlement developed around the confluence of the Rivers Cover, Skell, and Ure with the market square and the cathedral forming two quite distinct focal points. Either can be used as a starting point for a walk around the city but, as the latter is a building of such magnificence, it is perhaps best kept to the end as a grand finale.

The importance of Ripon derived in the first place from its religious connections, but it developed as a thriving market town because of its situation. To the west lie the sheep pastures of the dales, to the east the rich agricultural land of the Vale of York, and between lies Ripon with a ready-made transport route, the navigable River

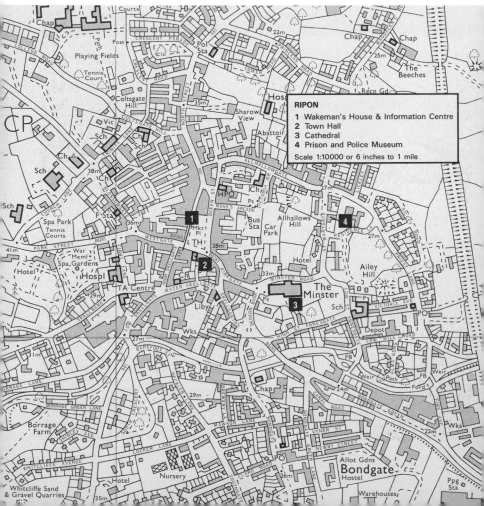

RIPON

1 Wakeman's House & Information Centre
2 Town Hall
3 Cathedral
4 Prison and Police Museum

Scale 1:10000 or 6 inches to 1 mile

Ure. Small wonder then that, when the famous writer, Daniel Defoe, came here in the early eighteenth century, he declared the market square to be the most beautiful in all England. Much of that attractiveness still remains, and the square still comes to life on market days. Each Thursday at 11 am the Ripon bellman rings in the official start of trading. The most prominent feature is the 90-ft high obelisk erected in 1781 to commemorate the fact that William Aislabie had been a Member of Parliament for sixty years. Of much more ancient significance is the sixteenth-century Wakeman's House (1) at the corner of the square. It was once the home of Hugh Ripley, the last Wakeman and the first Mayor of Ripon. The office of Wakeman was established in Saxon times, and the main function was to control the watch who guarded the city at night. Then James I called in at Ripon in 1617, and presented the city with a charter abolishing the old office, and replacing the Wakeman with a Mayor. But the old role has never been forgotten. At nine o'clock every evening, the Horn-blower in full regalia appears to blow the Wakeman's Horn at each corner of the square. No watch, however, answer the summons. The office is also recalled in a pious inscription on the classical Georgian town hall (2): 'Except Ye Lord keep Ye Cittie, Ye Wakeman Waketh in Vain'.

The old medieval streets, or 'Gates', that lead away from the Market Square may be a hindrance to traffic flow, but they have great charm and are still lined with a profusion of seventeenth- and eighteenth-century buildings. Kirkgate is the finest, not just for the street itself, but for its magnificent conclusion in the west front of the cathedral. The building has an air of massive solidity, heightened by the sombre gritstone of which it is built. It does have its fine decorative details — the elaborate geometrical tracery of the east window is a masterpiece of intersecting curves — but the memory that lingers is of a building that sits so firmly on the land that it seems almost to be a natural feature. Longevity is written in stone at Ripon, and nowhere is this more apparent than in the Saxon crypt, all that remains of the abbey founded in 669 by Bishop Wilfrid. The other great features of the church are the exquisite carvings on the stalls and misericords, the work of a famous school of carvers who worked in Ripon at the end of the fifteenth century.

By way of total contrast, one can leave the cathedral and walk up St Marygate, where the old Victorian prison cells have been converted into The Prison and Police Museum (4), telling

Ripon Cathedral, a splendid medieval building built on the site of a Saxon abbey.

Semer Water in the hills above Wensleydale.

the story of crime and punishment through the ages. Just to the south of the River Skell is the Ripon Canal, which is being restored so that boats will once again come right into the city. It leads away eastward past the racecourse on the Boroughbridge road. On **Tour 9**.

Rokeby Park (92) (NZ 0814) 2 miles SE of Barnard Castle
This is a splendid Palladian house of 1735, built by Sir Thomas Robinson for his own use and to his own design. The surrounding parkland was laid out shortly afterwards. It is a house with illustrious associations: as the setting for Scott's *Rokeby* ballad and as home, until 1905, of Velasquez' famous painting *The Rokeby Venus*. Its modern treasures include a unique collection of eighteenth-century needlework pictures. Across the Greta can be seen Mortham Tower, the fourteenth-century home of the Rokeby family. There is a small chapel by the A66, west of Rokeby Park, almost identical to Sir Thomas Robinson's chapel at Glynde in East Sussex.

The entrance to the park is on the minor road from Barnard Castle ★ to Greta Bridge ★ . On **Tour 8**.

Rylstone (103) (SD 9658) 5 miles N of Skipton
There is only a scattering of buildings on what was, in medieval times, the main road north from Skipton ★ , but they make a charming group. The houses stand among the trees, looking out on to a pond while the church is a little apart on the edge of the fell. The manor was home to the powerful Norton family, and the ruins of Norton Tower can be seen on a hill to the south. Wordsworth's poem, 'The White Doe of Rylstone' tells the legend of Francis Norton who was murdered and buried at Bolton Priory ★ . His sister took her pet doe to the grave and even after her death, it still came to the tomb.

Scar House Reservoir (98/99) (SD 0676) 9 miles NW of Pateley Bridge
An immense dam reaches right across upper Nidderdale to hold back the waters to create the reservoir. Work began in 1921 but was not completed until 1936, even though, at one time, 800 men were at work. The story is told in the museum in Pateley Bridge ★ . The dam is reached by a private road, which Yorkshire Water allows the public to use, from Lofthouse ★ . Can be visited by detour on **Tour 3**.

Sedbergh (97/98) (SD 6592)
Sedbergh sits just inside the western boundary of the National Park and, although Westminster moved it into Cumbria in 1974, its character is still essentially that of a market town of the Yorkshire Dales. The town is dominated by the brooding fells, and the busy rivers that flow down their valleys. It is a town predominantly built of local stone, with a main street behind which an intriguing maze of alleys invites exploration. Down one of these alleys, Weavers Yard, you can see an old house with a vast chimney, in which Bonnie Prince Charlie hid after the failure of the 1745 rebellion.

The church is Early English with heavy Victorian overtones, and nearby is the classically styled Grammar School of 1716, now a library. This represents one stage in the development of the Public School which has long since moved to a larger site to the south of the town. The main business of the town, however, has always been textiles, mainly woollens, though a cotton mill was built in the area. The tradition goes on. Fairfield Mill stands on the Hawes ★ road, approximately a mile from the town centre. In this Victorian woollen mill visitors can watch tweed being woven in fifty-year-old looms.

Sedbergh has been a centre of the Quaker faith since George Fox addressed 'a mighty meeting' here in 1652. In defiance of the law, the Quakers built a meeting house in the hamlet of Brigflatts. It has scarcely been changed since and can be seen, south of the A683, just outside the town.

Sedbergh is the starting point for **Tour 7**, but is also an excellent centre for walking and for exploring the Yorkshire Dales and the Cumbrian fells.

Semer Water (98) (SD 9287) 2 miles S of Bainbridge

Semer Water is a popular place for summer boating, but it is closed in winter to encourage migratory birds. Once a year, the Vicar of Askrigg ★ preaches from a boat. It features on **Tour 5** and **Walk 7**.

Settle (98) (SD 8163)

Settle is a small market town, but has always been a busy one, sat astride the main road from Yorkshire into Cumbria, at the point where it crosses the River Ribble. Its setting is as dramatic as of any town in the area, squashed into the space between the river and the hills with their shining crowns of limestone crags.

The market square is the natural focal point of the town. The arcaded building to the side was the old Shambles, occupied by butchers and the slaughter house. But there are plenty of other signs of a busy trading centre — look up above ground-floor level and you can see loading bays and hoists. Like many towns forced on to a restricted site, Settle has had to use all available space so that, behind the main streets, there is a complex of alleys and courtyards. The predominant theme of the town buildings is Georgian, that solidly respectable Georgian that characterises other northern towns such as Barnard Castle ★ and Richmond ★. But, scattered among them, are many buildings from the previous century, usually recognised by carved lintels and date stones. There are also two real oddities. 'The

Settle market. The town received its first market charter in the thirteenth century.

Folly' was built in 1675, though there is nothing to suggest how it got its name, unless it was disapproval of the splendid elaboration of its frontage. The local story has it that the builder ran out of funds and never completed it, but it is difficult to see what more could be added. The Naked Man Café in the Square is even more mysterious because no one seems to know why the carved — almost naked — man is there. There is a local history museum in Chapel Street. One thing Settle does not have is an ancient church. The local citizens went out through Kirkgate and across the river to Giggleswick ★.

For railway enthusiasts, Settle means the Settle and Carlisle Railway, which begins its long climb up the hills from its junction with the line to the coast at Settle Junction to the south of the town. Settle is the start of **Tour 2**.

Skipton (103) (SD 9851)

Skipton is an important market town, which began a new life at the end of the eighteenth century. The old elements are still there and plainly on view in the castle, the church, and the broad market square, which is in use almost throughout the week. Then the Leeds and Liverpool Canal arrived and, along its banks, grew up a new Skipton of wharves, warehouses, and mills, beyond which stretch Victorian terraces.

Far and away the most impressive feature in the town is the castle (**2**). The first castle was built soon after the Conquest, but little of the old remains. What we see today is largely the work of the Clifford family who took possession in 1309 and promptly set about building a new fortress. After the Civil War, that great restorer of the family property, Lady Anne Clifford set about the business of repairs and, over the following years, the castle developed two faces: that of the old grim fortress and the domesticity of the family home. The two sides appear as soon as you walk in for, just behind the massive round towers, is a little room decorated with shells. At the heart of the old castle is Conduit

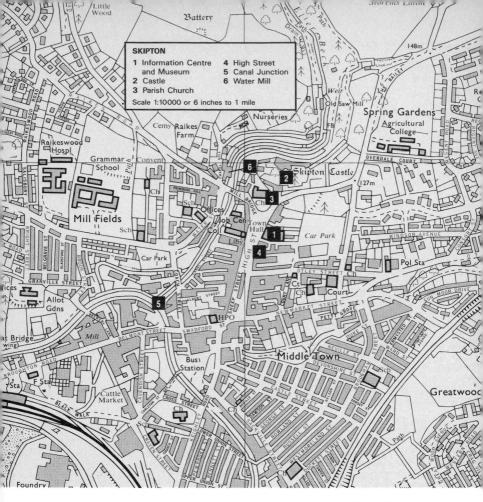

Court, with an ancient yew tree at its centre. Here again there is a contrast between the old fortifications and the more domestic note struck by Tudor builders. Altogether this is a quite splendid building.

Leaving the castle and turning to the town,

you find the church (3) standing at the end of the broad High Street (4) lined with market stalls. The church is largely Perpendicular, but additions and changes have been made over the years. The screen in front of the altar, for example, is a lovely carving of the late sixteenth century, but the painted, fussily gothic reredos beyond it is Gilbert Scott at his most pompous. Near the old north doorway is what appears to be a hermit's cell. Outside, the High Street is almost invariably busy with market traders. To the left is the Town Hall, with the local history museum and Information Centre (1). A number of narrow alleys lead off the High Street, one of which has recently been converted into a passable imitation of a Victorian market hall with an elaborate glass roof over a number of smart shops.

At the lower end, the High Street divides and becomes Sheep Street which, in turn, leads to Swadford Street. If you then turn right into Coach Street, you come to the canal at a point (5) where a short branch leads away past the castle,

Left: Skipton Castle, built mainly in the fourteenth century.

Right: Stainforth pack-horse bridge.

the Springs Branch. The old warehouses have now found new uses as shops and a boating centre. Away to the west are the dog-toothed silhouettes of loom sheds and the tall mill chimneys. The tow path of the Springs Branch provides a delightful walk which takes you back past the church and under the great cliff above which the high stone walls of the castle peer down. Beyond the castle, the canal ends by chutes which were used for loading stone from a nearby quarry. Here you can cross the stream which has accompanied the canal and walk towards the town. By the bridge is the old corn mill (**6**). Much of the building is now occupied by shops, but the old water-wheel and the mill machinery are still there, and it is hoped to open them to the public.

Skipton is a town of sturdy, robust qualities which will, with good fortune and good management, survive as it takes on a new role as a popular tourist centre, a 'Gateway to the Dales'. Start of **Tour 10** and on **Tour 2**.

Skyreholme (99) (SE 0660) 4 miles SE of Grassington
This tiny, scattered hamlet still divides itself into three parts, High, Middle, and just plain Skyreholme. Just to the north is Parcevall Hall, which is an ideal place to stop for a stroll. There are 16 acres of gardens and woodland with magnificent views over wild Dales country, and, well within walking distance, there is Troller's Gill, a limestone gorge almost as dramatic as Gordale Scar at Malham ★ but far less frequently visited. Skyreholme is a recommended stopping-off point on **Tour 2**.

Spennithorne (99) (SE 1389) 2 miles SE of Leyburn
A pleasant, comfortable village, Spennithorne has reminders of former glories. There are remnants — very scant remnants it must be admitted — of the Norman castle built by Ralph Fitz Randolph. The church, however, carries ample evidence of its ancient lineage. It was mentioned in Domesday, and three arches of the Norman church have survived successive rebuilding and restoration. It is a church full of fascinating details, from the sixteenth-century wall painting showing Time and Death to the splendid assortment of grotesque gargoyles. It also has one exotic touch — a Roman cross brought back from Sebastopol after the Crimean War.

Spofforth (104) (SE 3651) 3 miles SE of Harrogate
At first glance, this is just another pleasing village of sturdy, dark stone houses but, out on the western edge of the village, are the ruins of Spofforth Castle. The undercroft shows that there was a Norman castle here, but the buildings above ground are those of a fortified manor house. It is said that Harry Hotspur was born here. The church is also handsome, and in the churchyard is the grave of the famous road-builder, Blind Jack Metcalf of Knaresborough ★. **Tour 9** goes through Spofforth.

Stainforth (98) (SD 8267) 2 miles N of Settle
This modest village once stood on an important trade route between York ★ and Lancaster. The way crossed the Ribble on the narrow, high-

The Wolverine Cave, Stump Cross Caverns.

arched, seventeenth-century pack-horse bridge, now in the care of the National Trust. Below the bridge, the river dashes over the limestone ledges of Stainforth Force.

Starbotton (98) (SD 9574) 2 miles N of Kettlewell
There was a settlement recorded here in the Domesday Book, and there is still an air of antiquity about the place. Many of the fine stone houses and imposing barns have dates carved on the lintels showing that they were begun in the great rebuilding of the seventeenth century. There is a pub, The Fox and Hounds, a Quaker burial ground, and that seems all. But on the back road is a group of cottages, one of which is inscribed 'WS 1663 TS'. It is still possible to see that the cottages once formed one grand hall, home of an important local family, the Symond-sons. The rough road behind the village leads up to the remains of a lead smelting mill.

Studley Roger and **Studley Royal** see **Fountains Abbey**

An elegant stone house in Thoralby.

Stump Cross Caverns (99) (SE 0863) 4 miles W of Pateley Bridge
These limestone caves, now open to the public, were discovered by miners in 1860 — and take their name from the stump of the cross marking the boundary of the Forest of Knaresborough ★ . The main cave has beautiful stalactites and stalagmites, as well as remains of wolverines which roamed the area over 100,000 years ago and were found in the Wolverine Cave. The entrance is on the B6265 on **Tours 1** and **3**.

Swinithwaite (98) (SE 0489) 3 miles E of Aysgarth
Just south of the main road from the hamlet to Aysgarth ★ a little signpost points off to Templar's Chapel. Here are the remains of one of the old chapels of the Knights Templar — there is a boundary stone with their double cross insignia near the gate. Nearby, Temple Farm carries the initials of its builder, Peter Atkinson and his wife, and the date 1608. On **Tour 6**.

Tan Hill (91) (NY 9007) 7 miles E of Kirkby Stephen
The lonely inn on Stonesdale moor is the highest in England (1732 ft), and the Pennine Way goes past the door. Once it catered for the pack-horse trade and the coal miners working out on the moor. There is a sheep fair held up here each May. Those who are convinced the British climate is getting worse may care to know that it snowed here in both June and August 1880. **Tour 5** passes by.

Thoralby (98) (SE 0086) 1 mile S of Aysgarth
Thoralby lies on the northern slopes of Bishopdale, looking across the valley to Newbiggin ★ . There is a long main street and a neat triangular green, with a large number of fine

seventeenth-century houses, many with the traditional date carvings on the lintels. Thoralby is unusual in still having a working forge.

Thornton Rust (98) (SD 9788) 6 miles E of Hawes
Because it lies on a minor road which parallels the main road from Hawes ★ to Aysgarth ★ , Thornton Rust is a village which has been left peaceful and undisturbed. It has many typical stone houses with adjoining barns, but here many of the barns are two storeys high, with outside staircases, which gives a very distinctive air to this attractive village. On **Tour 5**.

Three Peaks
This is the popular name for the three highest hills in the Dales — Pen-y-ghent, Ingleborough, and Whernside. Enthusiastic walkers do all

One of the famous Three Peaks of the Dales: Pen-y-ghent seen from Dale Head.

three in a day; even more enthusiastic runners race the three. None, however, should be attempted by walkers unless they are experienced and properly equipped.

Threshfield (98) (SD 9963) 1 mile W of Grassington
Threshfield's most interesting building is some way from the village on the minor road that cuts across from Linton ★ to Grassington ★ . The

Threshfield School (below) was founded in 1674 as the Free Grammar School. The Manor (right) with its tall bay and circular window.

The rather formal cottages of Wensley show its origins as an estate village for Bolton Hall.

Free Grammar School, an attractive little building with a wide porch and mullioned windows, was founded in 1674 by Matthew Hewitt, rector of Linton. It is now a primary school. The village itself, being at a busy road junction, is easily ignored, but has a wealth of seventeenth-century houses and barns around the little green. Threshfield is on **Tour 2**.

Thwaite (98) (SD 8998) 5 miles N of Hawes
Thwaite stands at the foot of Butter Tubs Pass ★. It is one of those hamlets whose appeal lies in their complete lack of pretension, no more than a cluster of buildings snuggling together in a fold of the hills. The Pennine Way comes through here, but it is recommended as a stopping place on **Tour 5** for less ambitious walkers who can enjoy a stroll down the beautiful valley

of the Straw beck towards Muker ★.

Wensley (99) (SE 0989) 1 mile W of Leyburn
Once Wensley was a market town, grand enough to give its name to a whole valley. Now all that remains of those days is the old market cross in the churchyard. Wensley was devastated by plague in 1563 and never recovered, so that today it is a small but charming estate village for Bolton Hall ★. The church, however, is old and contains one quite remarkable feature, the private pew of the Bolton family. It looks for all the world like a box at Drury Lane, and local legend has it that this is no accident, but the work of the Third Duke who fell in love with and then married Lavinia Fenton, the actress who was the original Polly Peachum in *The Beggar's Opera*. **Walk 9** on **Tour 6** begins here.

Cheese

The name 'Wensleydale' is known to thousands for its famous cheese. It probably originated with the monks of Jervaulx Abbey, but was soon being made in individual farmhouses throughout the region. At first, ewe's milk was used but, by the seventeenth century, cows had become the main milk suppliers. The cows calved in the spring, and from then until the autumn, when they were at pasture, was the cheese-making time. The process is essentially simple. The milk was curdled using rennet, usually obtained from a calf's stomach lining. The milk would then separate into solid curds and liquid whey. The curd was squeezed and pressed to make

the cheese, which was then pickled in brine. Traditional Wensleydale could be blue or white.

In 1897, Edward Chapman bought in milk from the surrounding farms and began the first Wensleydale cheese factory in Hawes, and others followed in the area. In 1935 the Milk Marketing Board attempted to stop the production of Wensleydale cheese, but they were opposed by the doughty Kit Calvert who, with the help of local farmers, bought up and ran the Hawes Creamery. Today there are creameries in Hawes, Kirkby Malzeard, and Coverham, and Wensleydale has been joined by another traditional Yorkshire cheese, Coverdale.

West Burton (98) (SE 0186) 1 mile S of Aysgarth
This is one of the loveliest and least spoiled of all
the Wensleydale villages, tucked away on its
own along a road that leads only to a dead end
high in the hills. There is a wide, rectangular
green bordered by modest stone houses and
very little else. At the lower end of the village, a
path leads down to the waterfall on Walden
beck. It is a spot for those who appreciate peace
and quiet, dignified beauty, and it is surrounded
by a maze of footpaths, which is why it is recommended as a place to stop and stroll on **Tour 6**.

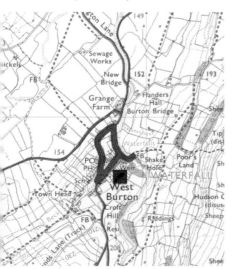

West Witton (98/99) (SE 0688) 4 miles W of
Leyburn
A long village, straggling out along the A684, it
has its moment of glory each year on the first
Saturday after St Bartholomew's Day. At dusk,

*Yockenthwaite, a tiny hamlet that seems to
epitomise all that is best in the Dales.*

the ceremony of 'Burning Owd Bartle' begins.
An effigy of Owd Bartle is carried through the
whole village while a traditional rhyme is
chanted:

At Pen Hill Crags he tore his rags;
At Hunter's Thorn he blew his horn;
At Capplebank Stee he brake his knee;
At Grisgill beck he brake his neck;
At Wadham's End he couldn't fend;
At Grisgill End he made his end.

And at Grass Gill End the effigy is finally burned.
No one seems to have any idea who Old Bartle
was, though there is presumably some connection with Bartholomew.
 A tower on the slopes of Penhill Beacon is a
monument erected by the Third Duke of Bolton,
in nearby Wensley ★ for his actress wife, and is
known as Polly Peachum Tower, after the character she originated. On **Tour 6**.

White Scar Caves (98) (SD 7174) 2 miles NE of
Ingleton
An impressive show cave, White Scar still has a
busy underground river running through it. The
entrance is on the B6255, between Ingleton ★
and Chapel-le-Dale ★ . On **Tour 4**.

Yockenthwaite (98) (SD 9079) 7 miles S of Hawes
A few old stone farmhouses and a pack-horse
bridge — that is all there is to Yockenthwaite,
apart from a river that burbles and bounces over
a series of little falls between the hills that rise
around Langstrothdale. This is a lovely spot for
walking or, as many people have discovered,
picnicking by the river while the children paddle.
Walk 10 on **Tour 6** passes through the hamlet.

York

A walk around the city

York is a chequerboard of eight successive cities, intermingled above ground and piled layer on layer beneath, like the tiers of a rich cake; excavate almost anywhere within its walls, and you cut through twenty centuries of history. At the foundation lies Roman Eboracum, military headquarters of Roman Britain; next comes Anglo-Saxon Eoforwic, ecclesiastical capital of the Christian north; then prosperous Viking Jorvik, which became proud medieval York, second city of Plantagenet England. Above again lies Tudor and Stuart York, the 'metropolis of the north', torn between Royalist and Parliamentarian; and then fashionable Georgian York, with its races, assemblies, and opulent town mansions. Then, very near the surface, comes the workaday Victorian city of railways and chocolate works; and finally busy modern York, which has assured its present and future by preserving so much of its past.

The strata of York's history are most strikingly seen near the Anglian Tower (2), where this tour begins: here the bank of the city wall has been cut away to reveal four successive layers of ramparts, medieval on Norman on Viking on Roman. The Anglian Tower itself, built of rough masonry to plug a gap in the Roman wall, belongs to the obscure centuries between Romans and Vikings, and is the only surviving fortification of this period in England.

Much more impressive is the nearby Multiangular Tower, at the western corner of the Roman defences, which still stands to its full height. It was altered in medieval times, the division between the neat Roman masonry and the more haphazard later additions being clearly visible. The tower was originally raised by the Roman general Constantius in about AD 300, soon after he had suppressed a British independence movement: seven more such bastions once lined the river front of the fortress, a show of strength doubtless intended to overawe recalcitrant Britons (whose settlement lay on the opposite bank) with the unconquerable might of Rome.

The external face of the tower can be seen by passing through an adjacent door into the grounds of St Mary's Abbey (3), now the Museum Gardens. St Mary's was one of the largest and wealthiest Benedictine monasteries of the north, and some shadow of its magnificence survives in the ruined west end of its church, built during the thirteenth century and originally 360 feet long, or nearly three-quarters of the size of the Minster. Every four years it forms a dramatic backdrop for the famous York Mystery Plays. The timber-framed monastic guest house still stands by the river, and portions of the monks' living quarters can be seen in the basement of the Georgian Yorkshire Museum (4) — which also houses a fascinating collection of prehistoric, Roman, and Viking finds. Behind the museum (and accessible via a passage near the city wall) is red-brick and stone King's Manor (5) with its quiet courtyards and Elizabethan interiors. Once the residence of the abbots of St Mary's, under Henry VIII, it became the headquarters of the King's Council in the North.

Leaving the Museum Gardens by the main entrance, the west front of the Minster immediately dominates the skyline. On the way, a short detour down Blake Street reaches the Assembly Rooms (6) designed by the aristocratic architect Lord Burlington in 1730. Its cavernous Classical interior witnessed the glittering entertainments of fashionable Georgian York, notorious for its unscrupulous heiress hunters. By the Minster (7), turn left into narrow High Petergate (8), and ascend the city wall at medieval Bootham Bar (9), the north-west gate of the city. Its windows look out on to the Art Gallery (10) and down Bootham, a street which owes its Georgian character to rebuilding after the great Civil War siege of 1644.

The section of wall beginning here is the most impressive in York, with panoramic views of the Minster and its attendant buildings, notably the Minster Library, a former thirteenth-century chapel packed with ancient books and documents. At the turning of the wall, Rowntree's cocoa and chocolate works, a major York employer since Victorian times, can be clearly seen in the distance. Then the wall (now fronted by a deep, dry ditch) continues along Lord Mayor's Walk to Monk Bar (11), the north-east gate, topped by menacing sculptured figures eternally hurling stones at would-be attackers.

Thereafter, the defences extend (via a much less spectacular section) to Peasholme Green — once the site of a marshy pool, unsuitable for wall-building and, in any case, impenetrable to assault — and they resume again at the Red Tower in Foss Islands Road (12). It is therefore better to descend at Monk Bar into Goodramgate, one of York's Scandinavian gatas (or streets) named after a Viking resident called Guthrum. After passing a lane named Ogleforth ('the owls' ford'), Goodramgate opens to the right on to a sudden close-up view of the east end of the Minster with St William's College (13) opposite. The largest timber-framed building in York, this mainly fifteenth-century hall once housed the twenty-eight chantry priests who served the Minster's lesser altars. Beyond it is the Treasurer's House (14), a dignified seventeenth-century gabled mansion, giving the impression of having been transported from some rural estate.

After the gap, Goodramgate continues past

A reconstructed street in York Castle Museum, decked out for Jubilee celebrations.

Clifford's Tower, the keep of York Castle. It stands on the motte of the Norman original.

Our Lady's Row, the oldest occupied houses in the city. These were built for the fourteenth-century priests of Holy Trinity Goodramgate, which hides immediately behind them in its little churchyard. One of York's lesser-known treasures, its outer shell is medieval, but it is most memorable for its charming 'Prayer Book' interior, packed with high Stuart and Georgian box pews, and dominated by a two-decker pulpit: generally, such fittings were swept away by Victorian 'restorers'.

Goodramgate finally emerges into King's Square, the centre of the ancient city and probably the site of its Viking royal palace, home of the notorious Erik Bloodaxe and other rulers of Scandinavian Jorvik. In later times it became the focus of the market district, and a turn left here reveals the Shambles (**15**), York's most famous thoroughfare. Here, the city butchers had their 'shammels', or meat counters. The jumbled timber-framed houses lean over almost to touch across the street. Today, the Shambles is full of souvenir shops but, immediately behind it, York's bustling vegetable and general market still cheerfully and noisily operates six days a week, as it has done here for over 700 years.

On the far side of the market runs broad Parliament Street, site of York's great annual fairs until the 1920s. Almost opposite the lane from the market stand three tall painted brick houses, with ominous cracks between them — they were built across the inadequately filled Roman defensive ditch, and, over the centuries, have settled into it.

Parliament Street ends at the church of All Saints Pavement, with its graceful lantern tower: this is the parish church of York's ancient trade guilds, whose ceremonial services continue to be held here. A few hundred yards beyond it, on Picadilly, is the splendid medieval Merchant Adventurers' Hall (**16**), still the home of the largest and richest of the guilds whose prosperity sprang from trading Yorkshire wool for Baltic furs and French wine. The hall backs on to Fossgate which leads, after a longish walk, to Walmgate Bar (**17**), the south-east gate of the

city and the only one to retain its barbican or outer gate, still pitted with the bullet scars of the Civil War siege.

Immediately adjacent to All Saints Church, off Coppergate, is an area which epitomises York's many-layered history — a brand-new shopping centre built above one of the city's most ancient trading streets. Excavations for the new Coppergate centre revealed the remarkably well-preserved remains of Scandinavian houses and workshops, the manufacturing core of Viking Jorvik; these are now imaginatively displayed beneath the complex in the Jorvik Viking Centre (**18**), where visitors are borne in 'time-cars' through the sights, sounds, and even smells of the Viking town.

Nor is this the only attraction of the area for, just beyond, is the York Story (**19**), an audio-visual display within the old church of St Mary Castlegate. In Castlegate itself is Fairfax House (**20**), a noble Georgian town house with a wealth of fine furniture and interiors. Castlegate leads to another great York star, the Castle Museum (**21**), housed in two vast Georgian blocks once used as prisons. Dick Turpin, the highwayman, was held in the condemned cell here, but the principal attractions are two complete streets of fully stocked Georgian and Victorian shops, rescued from demolition and re-erected within the museum.

Protected on three sides by the Rivers Ouse and Foss, York's castle was once one of the key fortresses of the north, and its most spectacular survival is Clifford's Tower (**22**): this was begun in the 1240s as the keep or strongpoint of the castle, its four-leafed clover shape being unique in Britain. It stands on a precipitous, steep-sided mound first raised by William the Conqueror in 1068-69, and is the fourth successive keep on the site. Within one of its predecessors, in 1190, the entire Jewish population of York committed suicide to avoid falling into the hands of antisemitic local 'crusaders'.

The Conqueror did not deem one castle suffi-

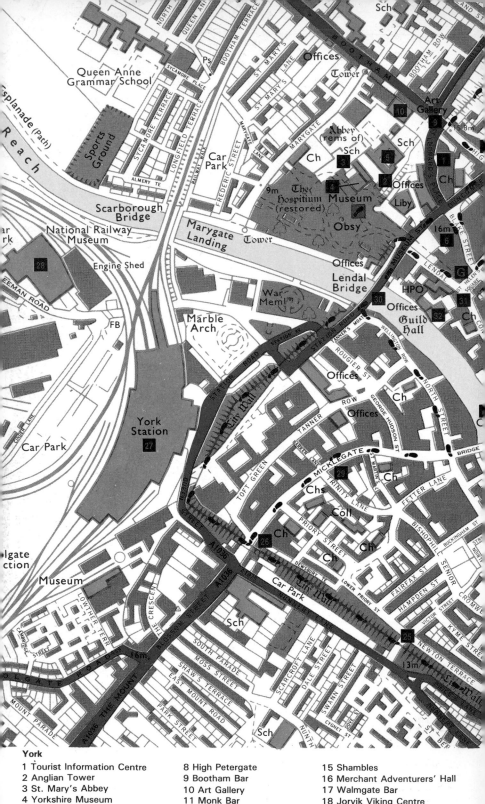

York

1 Tourist Information Centre
2 Anglian Tower
3 St. Mary's Abbey
4 Yorkshire Museum
5 Kings Manor
6 Assembly Rooms
7 Minster

8 High Petergate
9 Bootham Bar
10 Art Gallery
11 Monk Bar
12 Foss Islands Road
13 St. William's College
14 Treasurer's House

15 Shambles
16 Merchant Adventurers' Hall
17 Walmgate Bar
18 Jorvik Viking Centre
19 York Story
20 Fairfax House
21 York Castle Museum

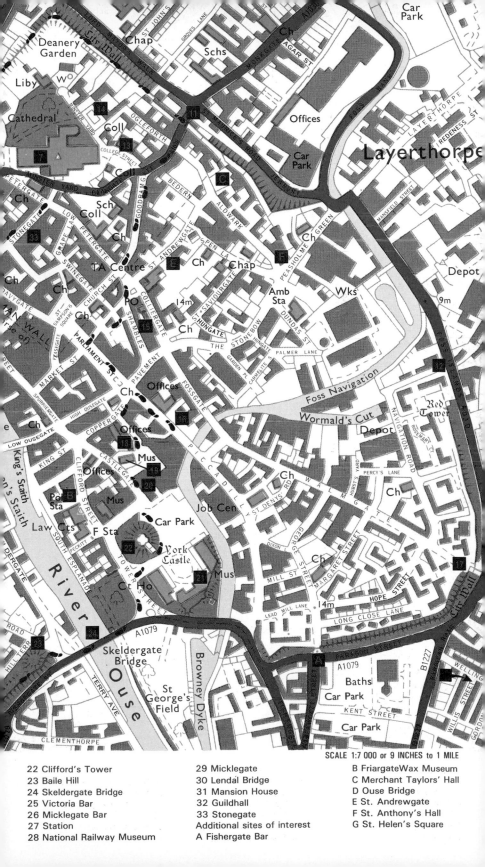

SCALE 1:7 000 or 9 INCHES to 1 MILE

22 Clifford's Tower
23 Baile Hill
24 Skeldergate Bridge
25 Victoria Bar
26 Micklegate Bar
27 Station
28 National Railway Museum

29 Micklegate
30 Lendal Bridge
31 Mansion House
32 Guildhall
33 Stonegate
Additional sites of interest
A Fishergate Bar

B FriargateWax Museum
C Merchant Taylors' Hall
D Ouse Bridge
E St. Andrewgate
F St. Anthony's Hall
G St. Helen's Square

cient to control the unruly York citizens, who were only too happy to welcome raiding parties of their Scandinavian cousins. To close the Ouse against Viking longships, he built a second stronghold on the opposite bank, and this fortress — now a tree-grown mound called Baile Hill (**23**) — can be reached by crossing Victorian Skeldergate Bridge (**24**) and mounting the city wall. After skirting around Baile Hill, this section of the wall encloses the now-fashionable Victorian terraces of Bishophill: to the right from near Victoria Bar (**25**), can be glimpsed the Anglo-Saxon tower of St Mary Bishophill Junior, York's oldest parish church.

Next comes Micklegate Bar (**26**), the south-western gate of the city and the most impressive of them all — probably because it looks down the main road from London, and it was here that York's civic dignitaries customarily welcomed visiting monarchs coming from the capital. Outside it stands the Bar Convent Museum of Roman Catholicism in York, displaying a splendid Classical chapel (with priest's hole) and relics of local Catholics who suffered for their faith. Many of them died on the Knavesmire, a mile or so further down the London road. Now the site of York's famous garden racecourse, this was once the execution place of the city's felons or 'knaves'.

At this point, visitors have the choice of continuing round the wall to Lendal Bridge or making an interesting detour down Micklegate. Railway enthusiasts should stay on the wall; those interested in churches should opt for Micklegate.

From Micklegate Bar, a particularly high stretch of wall continues to Lendal Bridge, providing fine distant views of the Minster. To the right it passes the massive modern railway offices, partly built on the site of York's first station of 1840, the deserted platforms of which can still be seen. This was the creation of George Hudson 'the Railway King' — entrepreneur, three times Lord Mayor of York, and finally (when the awesome extent of his corruption, bullying, and fraud was exposed) disgraced crook.

Opposite, but outside the wall, is the present station (**27**) of 1877, renowned for its breathtaking 800 feet of curved roof-tunnel in ornate Victorian ironwork. Behind it stretch acres of sidings and carriage works, a reminder of the continuing importance of railways in York's history. It is fitting that Britain's National Railway Museum (**28**), with its unrivalled collection of historic locomotives, should be sited a short walk from the station. During summer weekends, one of its veteran locomotives can often be seen 'in steam', preparing to haul a train full of enthusiasts to Scarborough.

Micklegate (**29**) itself is not to be missed. Its name, appropriately, means 'the great street', and it is probably the stateliest in the city. Curving down a hill (one of the few in level York), it passes some exceptionally grand Georgian mansions, as well as the much-altered priory church of Holy Trinity — near the east end of which, on Trinity Lane, is the charming timber-framed house called Jacob's Well. At the foot of Micklegate hill, opposite the street recently renamed after George Hudson (York has always had a sneaking admiration for the old repro-

bate), is another part-medieval church, St Martin-cum-Gregory, and farther on to the left yet another, St John's (now the Arts Centre) with its pretty brick and timber tower.

The most fascinating of all the city's many parish churches is reached by turning left here into North Street, where slender-spired All Saints and its attendant timbered cottages face the red-brick colossus of the Viking Hotel. Lining its atmospheric interior is York's finest display of stained-glass windows outside the Minster — notably the second from the east on the north side, wherein a long-bearded benefactor distributes charity to crippled beggars and pilloried prisoners. The next window to the east depicts the end of the world as a fifteenth-century strip cartoon, and across the church a hierarchy of glass angels lead popes, kings, and citizens (one wearing medieval spectacles) into heaven. Flanking the roof above — recently and controversially repainted in glowing colours — are more angels playing musical instruments.

Across the Ouse from All Saints is the long, battlemented river front of the Guildhall, with the dark barred archway of its watergate below. This watergate marks the crossing point of the long-vanished Roman bridge, and, from it, an underground passage — York's oldest thoroughfare — follows the line of the Roman road beneath the Guildhall, to emerge above ground as Stonegate and head straight for the place that was once the Roman headquarters building, and is now the Minster.

To trace its course, cross Victorian Lendal Bridge (**30**) and turn right down Lendal to the crimson-painted Mansion House (**31**), begun in 1726 as the official residence of York's Lord Mayors. Every Lord Mayor still moves in during his year of office, to enjoy the services of its butler and cook, and the use of its magnificent state room for official functions. There, too, are guarded the city's ancient silver mace and great medieval two-handed sword, always borne before the Lord Mayor in civic processions and represented in the city's heraldic arms, together with the scarlet and ermine 'cap of maintenance'. They proclaim York's proud status as a county in its own right, granted by King Richard II in 1396.

Immediately behind the Mansion House (via an archway) is the Guildhall (**32**), not only the nerve centre of York's government for five centuries, but also — as flame-scorched masonry underlines — a symbol of its indomitable spirit. Built during the 1440s, in 1942 the hall was gutted by German incendiary bombs. It burned uncontrollably for twelve hours but, even before the fires died down, the decision was taken to reconstruct it in its original form. The only variation is the window depicting the great events of York's long history.

That history is characterised by Stonegate (**33**), the street connecting the Guildhall with the Minster, the civic and the spiritual focus of the city. The Via Praetoria or imperial way of Roman Eboracum, the *steingata* or stone-paved street of Viking Jorvik, it is a patchwork of Norman, medieval, Stuart, Georgian, and Victorian houses, interspersed with the shop fronts of modern York — the 2,000-year-old city, the story of which is the story of England.

York Minster

The Minster is entered from the west door which leads into the nave: this part of the cathedral was begun in 1291 and completed in the 1350s. If you walk to the centre of the nave and turn to face the door you have entered, you will see above it the great west window which dates from 1338. Above the left corner is the south-west tower which has a peal of twelve bells. York's medieval brass foundry was in the area known as Bedern — a passage off St Andrewgate. Archaeologists have discovered furnaces and the remains of clay moulds for the bells. Above the right corner is the north-west tower which houses Great Peter, a 16-ton bell which has the deepest tone of any bell in Europe.

In York Minster's nave, if you look up — and above all else, gothic architecture is designed to make you do that — you will see that it is decorated with shields high up on the stonework on either side. These depict the arms of the benefactors of the Minster and the barons who fought in the long wars against Scotland. In 1314 Edward II and his nobles prayed for victory at the cathedral on their way to the Battle of Bannockburn. Their prayers were in vain, but their shields can be seen in the clerestory windows.

Walking down the nave to the crossing and transepts gives the visitor the best view of the Minster's stained glass. The great west window, now being restored, is known from its heart-shaped stone tracery as the 'heart of Yorkshire', and depicts some of the principal events in the life of Christ. These events were included in York's famous Mystery Plays which told the Bible story from the Creation to the Last Judgment. Originally, they were performed by the city's craft guilds — also known as 'masteries' or 'mysteries' — and it is recorded that they were performed for Richard III, England's last truly northern king, and not as bad as the Tudors painted him.

One of the cathedral's greatest glories is its glass. The north transept contains one of the most beautiful stained-glass windows in the world, 'The Five Sisters'. Each of the thirteenth-century lancet windows is over 50 feet tall and glazed with grey-green 'grisaille' glass. The beauty of the design made an impression on Sir Basil Spence (architect of Coventry Cathedral) that was to stay with him throughout his career. The windows inspired Charles Dickens to write a story about its origin in Nicholas Nickleby. Another chapter in York's history is recalled by the devotion of two women of the city who organised the re-leading of 'The Five Sisters' window in 1925 with medieval lead found at Rievaulx Abbey. All works of art need repair, and their work was dedicated to making the window a memorial to all the women of the Empire who died in the Great War. The astronomical clock to the right of the window in the north transept is a memorial to the 18,000 men of the RAF and other air forces stationed in the north who lost their lives in World War II.

In the south transept is the famous Rose Window which is said to commemorate the marriage of Henry VII and Elizabeth of York and the end of the Wars of the Roses. Ironically, the window celebrates an event which marked a turn in York's fortunes. For, under the Tudors, the all-important wool industry went into a sharp decline, and there were outbreaks of epidemic witnessed by plague pits which have been found in the city.

At the east end of the Minster is the east window, physically the most impressive work of the medieval glaziers whose workshops were situated in the area of present-day St Helen's Square. The window is the size of a tennis court and takes as its theme the Latin quotation at the apex: Ego Sum, Alpha et Omega — 'I am the Beginning and the End'.

It is not possible to list all the treasures of York Minster here, nor is it important to do so. What is important is for the visitor to understand that this is the heart of York: the Minster is the spiritual centre of the city and the repository of an infinite number of clues to its long history. Several times fire has threatened to destroy the building: when a deranged man, called Jonathan Martin, set fire to hymn and prayer books after evensong in 1829 (he died in Bedlam); when a careless workman left a candle alight in the south-west tower; and in 1984 when it was struck by lightning. Still York Minster survived.

Tour 1
Pateley Bridge and
Bolton Abbey

39 miles. This tour starts in Pateley Bridge and at once climbs up on to the high moorland which will be a feature for much of the journey. It then turns down Wharfedale past the beautiful site of Bolton Priory, before setting off on a lonely moorland road. There is a visit to the artificial lakes of Fewston and Swinsty Reservoirs, and the final stage of the journey is down country lanes at the edge of the Dales. All tours in the Dales have hills but cyclists will find this route easier than most. Pateley Bridge in many ways is a typical small town of the millstone grit region. It stretches up a steep hill, its dark stone houses interlaced with little alleys and courtyards, and the overall darkness is relieved by the flowers than can be seen everywhere in the town.

Leave Pateley Bridge ★ on the B6265 Grassington ★ Road, which crosses the River Nidd and then climbs up the long, steep hill to Bewerley Moor. The first part of the journey is also followed in **Tour 3**. As you climb, so the views become ever wider, and a steady succession of hills and valleys stretch far into the distance.

At Greenhow Hill ★ is the pub, The Miners Arms, a good clue to the importance that this area once held. On each side of the road, you can see the humps and hollows that mark the work of the lead miners. Beyond the village the road crosses into the Dales National Park on the open expanses of Craven Moor. On the left is the entrance to Stump Cross Caverns ★. These natural caves were discovered by two miners in 1860 and are now open to the public. The main cave has an air of fantasy, with its stalagmites and stalactites coloured by concealed lighting.

The road continues through the heather-covered moorland and, just beyond Dibbles Bridge, over the River Dibb, turn left **(A)** on to the minor road, signposted to Burnsall ★. At the T-junction turn right. Burnsall is a place for a suggested stroll, and there is a car park near the bridge. This attractive village has a notice board on the green, pointing out places of interest and there is a pleasant walk down to the river. The tour crosses the bridge and turns left **(B)** on to the B6160 signposted to Bolton Abbey ★. The road now runs down Wharfedale, past the gaunt ruins of Barden Tower ★. A mile further on there is a parking space where you can leave the car for a walk to the river to see the

The River Wharfe above Bolton Abbey is forced through this narrow gap in the rocks known as The Strid.

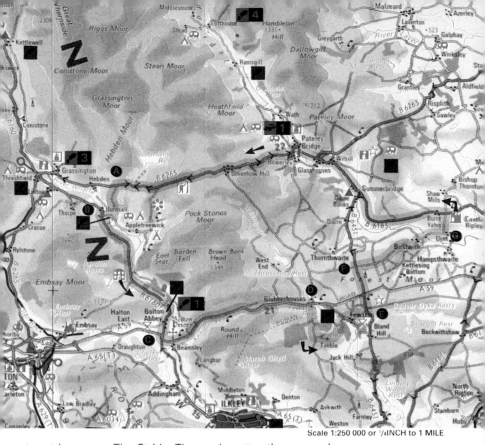

cataract known as The Strid. The road continues on to Bolton Abbey, where there is a car park on the right. Here you can park either to stroll down to see the priory in its beautiful setting on a bend of the river, or take **Walk 1** which goes along the valley visiting both The Strid and Barden Tower. After the pause, continue on along the B6160 to the A59, where you turn to the left **(C)**.

One mile after the turning, after the road has widened to allow an extra lane up the hill, look out on the left-hand side for the almshouses of Beamsley ★ Hospital, recognised by the coat of arms over the archway. Beyond the arch is a circular building, where the living rooms radiate out from a central chapel. Beyond Beamsley Hospital, the road crosses Beamsley Moor and Blubberhouses Moor. It passes through a narrow, twisting valley where the dark stone appears as craggy outcrops. The road comes down towards the village of Blubberhouses ★ ; turn right by the church on to the minor road signposted to Otley ★ **(D)**. At the top of the hill turn left to-Timble, and, where the road divides, take the right fork to the village. A mile beyond the village there is a car park where you can stop for a stroll by the two

attractive reservoirs.

After the car park, turn right at the junction to cross between the reservoirs. The road bends to the right and then divides. Take the left fork and continue on to the B6451. Turn left **(E)** and continue straight on across the A59 past the giant 'golf balls' of the RAF radar installation. Turn right at the crossroads **(F)** on the road to Birstwith. This is a pleasant road with good views on either side. A large, imposing building on the left-hand side of the road, set back on a hill top overlooking the Nidd is Swarcliffe Hall. Charlotte Brontë spent three unhappy weeks in the house that once stood on this site, when she was a governess. As you reach Birstwith, the road does a dog leg, turning first right, then left, to cross the Nidd. Beyond the river the road bends round to the right to join the B6165. Turn left to Burnt Yates **(G)** — the route here has briefly joined that of **Tour 9**. Continue on the B6165. This route has now returned to the lead mining area where villages have such significant names as Smelthouses and Glasshouses and, rather surprisingly, New York. Continue on this attractive route along the valley of the Nidd back to Pateley Bridge.

Tour 2
Settle, Skipton, and the Limestone Spectaculars

61 miles. The first part of the tour skirts the edge of the Dales between Settle and Skipton, but then turns north for the very heart of the region. It passes through the popular and delightful town of Grassington and then follows lonely valley roads to the most exciting scenery of the whole area, centred on the village of Malham. It is a route which can be said to sample all the delights the Dales have to offer. Cyclists may find the main road sections to be carrying heavy traffic.

Scale 1:250 000 or ¼INCH to 1 MILE

Leave Settle ★ on the A65 heading south along the broad Ribble valley to Long Preston ★. Take the second main right turn (A) on to the A682 signposted to Nelson. Over to the right there are fine views across to the hills of the Forest of Bowland. Three miles beyond Long Preston turn left on to a minor road (B) signposted to Gargrave ★. It passes through a pleasant landscape of grassy hillocks. After 2 miles turn left and continue on to Bank Newton ★, where the road is joined by the Leeds and Liverpool Canal. There are parking spaces here, where you can stop for a stroll along the tow-path to watch the boats going through Bank Newton locks. The road crosses the canal a little way further on at Priest Holme Bridge and then passes under the railway and continues on into Gargrave. At the T-junction at the edge of town, turn left

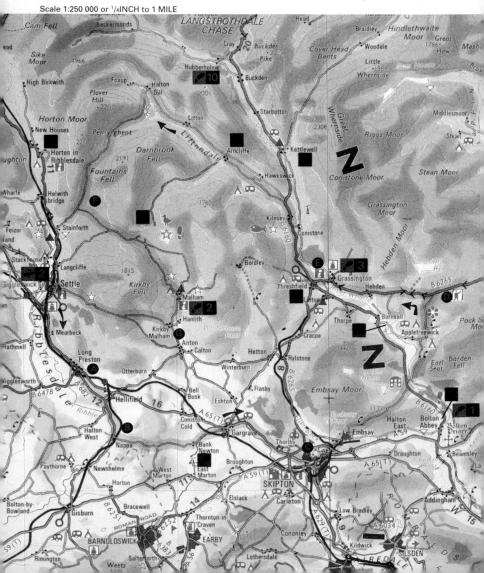

across the River Aire and, at the main road beyond the bridge, turn right on to the A65 to Skipton ★ .

The A65 meets the Skipton bypass at a roundabout. Take the second turning signposted to Skipton. Skipton is a town to explore with its fine castle, busy market, and many attractive buildings. It is also the starting point for **Tour 10**. The through route crosses the canal by an old corn mill, and, at the end of the Market Place, turn left on to the A6131, past the church and the castle. The road bends round up the hill. Turn left **(C)** on to the minor road signposted to Embsay ★ and Eastby. In the middle of Embsay there is a sign on the right for the Yorkshire Dales Railway, a little preserved steam railway that prides itself on its friendliness and caters for the whole family. At the end of the village turn left for Eastby. The road now climbs up to the heather moors, where the rocky outcrops are, for once, not limestone but millstone grit. There are fine views to the right over Wharfedale.

At the B6160 turn left to pass the romantic ruins of Barden Tower ★ , a former hunting lodge, where you turn right across the River Wharfe on a minor road signposted to Appletreewick ★ . Where the road bends sharply left, take the minor road to the right, signposted to Pateley Bridge ★ . Where the road turns through a hairpin, there is a turning to Parcevall Hall ★ . This is a lovely spot where it is possible to stroll through the grounds of the Elizabethan house and walk to the dramatic rocky gorge, Trollers Gill. Those who take the detour must retrace their steps to rejoin the principal route back at the hairpin bend. At the road junction **(D)** turn left on to the B6265 along the southern edge of Hebden Moor to Grassington ★ . This is the starting point for **Walk 3** and **Tour 3**. The road turns left in the town to cross the River Wharfe to Threshfield ★ **(E)**. Turn right on to the B6160 signposted to Kettlewell ★ . The road passes under the shadow of the imposing overhanging crag at Kilnsey ★ . One mile after the village of Kilnsey, turn left on to the minor road signposted Arncliffe ★ . This attractive village with its central green is a suggested stopping place for a stroll down to the church and the river.

The road bends to the left towards Littondale and Litton ★ . This whole valley is a delight, typifying the best of Dales scenery, and reaches a suitable finale at Halton Gill ★ , huddled into the fold of the hills. The road turns left here and climbs steeply up the hillside to provide superb views

The old mill beside the Springs Branch of the Leeds and Liverpool Canal at Skipton.

across Littondale. This is a very lonely switchback road running high above the little river valley to the left and dominated by the peak of Pen-y-ghent to the right. Six miles from Halton Gill turn left on the minor road signposted Malham ★ **(F)**. Two-and-a-half miles along the road there is a left turn to Malham Tarn, and shortly beyond that a crossroads. The road that goes straight on takes you to a parking place, just beyond Malham beck, from where you can stroll to the tarn. The main route goes to the right, heading down into the village of Malham. Along the way, look out on the left-hand side for the spectacular cliff Malham Cove and the strange limestone pavement above it. In Malham itself there is car parking at the National Park Centre which is the starting point for **Walk 2**.

Follow the road to Kirkby Malham ★ with its surprisingly large and impressive church **(G)** and bear right to cross Scosthrop Moor. At the T-junction, turn right and return to Settle through a final example of superb limestone scenery.

Tour 3 Wharfedale, Nidderdale, and Coverdale

50 miles. This tour begins in Wharfedale and crosses the moors to Nidderdale, the most easterly of the dales; not perhaps as popular as some of the other valleys, but it is every bit as beautiful. From here there is another crossing of high moorland to the ruins of Jervaulx Abbey. The route continues through the wild scenery of Coverdale to Kettlewell, where it rejoins Wharfedale. This is very much a route for those who delight in wild moorland scenery. Cyclists will find some particularly steep hills on this route. The route starts in Grassington, one of the show places of the Dales, with its steep, cobbled streets climbing up the valley side towards the wild moors. This is the starting point for **Walk 3**.

Leave Grassington ★ on the B6265 towards Pateley Bridge ★ . The road passes across the deep valley of the Hebden beck, where the village stretches away as a long line of stone houses to the right. This first part of the route is also included in **Tour 2**. The majority of the section beyond Hebden ★ is described in **Tour 1**. The road goes very steeply downhill and, just before reaching the bridge over the Nidd at Pateley Bridge, turn left by the garage on the minor road signposted to Wath and Lofthouse ★ **(A)**.

The road now follows the Nidd Valley northwards. One mile along the road you pass the Watermill Inn on your left. The building was originally Foster Beck Mill where flax was spun for the linen indus-

try, and the huge water-wheel that powered the machinery can still be seen at the end of the building. The road winds past Gouthwaite Reservoir ★ which, although artificial, has something of the appearance of a Scottish loch. It is a favourite spot for birdwatchers: 200 different species have been recorded, and in winter, whooper swans are a common sight. At the end of the reservoir is the pleasant village of Ramsgill ★ , its village green dominated by an immense chestnut tree. You can stop here for a stroll across the head of the reservoir to Bouthwaite.

Continue up the narrowing valley to the point where the road divides **(B)** and take the right-hand fork to Lofthouse ★ . This lovely old village is the starting point for **Walk 4**. The road now climbs very steeply up to an area of wild heather-covered moorland, and crosses the end of Leighton ★ reservoir. The road goes downhill to cross the River Burn and then bends round to the right. Just before the village of Healey, turn left **(C)** on the minor road signposted to Ellingstring. The scenery is now very different; a gentle landscape of fields and hedgerows takes over from the rough moorland and dry stone walls. After 2 miles, turn left at the crossroads to Jervaulx Abbey ★ . At the junction **(D)** turn left on to the A6108 and the car park for Jervaulx Abbey is on the left. The abbey may not be as picturesque as Fountains ★ or Bolton Priory ★ , but it gives a very clear idea of the extent and nature of one of the great monasteries.

Continue on the main road to East Witton ★ and, where the main road turns sharp right, continue straight on up the wide village street. You are now back in the Dales National Park, a fact which is

Some say that Gouthwaite Reservoir has improved the scenery; this can not be claimed for the squares of conifers on the hills.

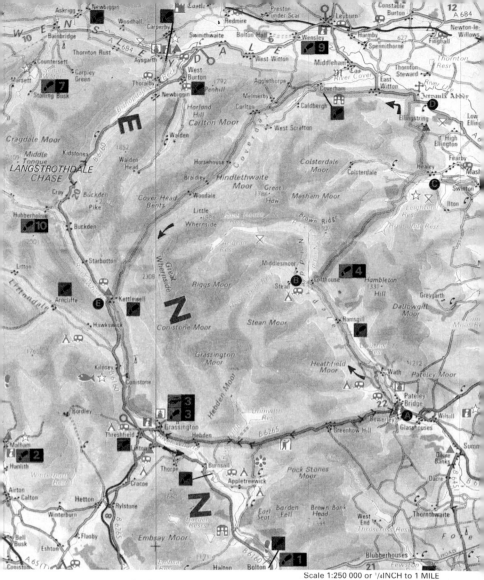

very soon reflected in the scenery on the left. You pass the seventeenth-century farmhouse, Braithwaite Hall, which is owned by the National Trust, but which can only be visited by special appointment. Cross Coverham ★ Bridge. The road bends left and then right to a T-junction, where you turn left to continue the tour. However, there is a suggested stroll to Coverham Abbey, for which you turn right and park on the green by the pond. The main route now continues down Coverdale, passing through the long, straggling village of Carlton ★. This is a beautiful and remote valley, with only a scattering of hamlets. At the very head of the dale, just before the road drops steeply down into Kettlewell ★, look out

on the right-hand side for Hunters Stone ★, a tall stone incised with a small cross which marked the route from Coverham Abbey to Kettlewell ★.

Kettlewell (E) which, like Grassington, was once an important lead mining centre, is a pleasant spot to pause and stroll through the village and along the river bank. Continue the tour by taking the left turn in the village signposted to Skipton ★, then turn left again, before crossing the bridge, on to the road signposted to Conistone ★. The road follows the River Wharfe and gives a fine view across to Kilnsey ★ Crag. At Conistone turn left, passing Grass Wood, where there are footpaths to be explored, to return to Grassington.

Tour 4
Kirkby Lonsdale, The Limestone Peaks, and Peaceful Dentdale

The playing fields of Sedbergh School.

52 miles. The tour begins at Kirkby Lonsdale, but could begin at Hawes (B) or Sedbergh (E). It offers a great variety of scenery, varying from the peaceful area of upper Dentdale to the high moors and limestone escarpments of the Three Peaks. It crosses and re-crosses the line of the Settle and Carlisle Railway. Towns met along the way are as varied as the wild scenery; Kirkby Lonsdale, itself an elegant market town, contrasts with the narrow cobbled streets of Dent, one of the most attractive towns in the whole of the Dales. The roads are equally varied, ranging from A roads to steep and winding single-track roads. Cyclists who follow this route will find it very hilly and strenuous. The tour starts at Kirkby Lonsdale ★, where there is a recommended stroll from the town to the river and the Devil's Bridge.

Leave the town on the A65 (T), heading south towards Settle ★ . The road crosses the Leck beck at Cowan Bridge ★ where the Brontë children were sent to school. All the time, as you travel south, the view is increasingly dominated by the great flat-topped hill of Ingleborough. Cross the bridge over the River Greta on the outskirts of Ingleton H **(A)**, then turn left on to the B6255. This is a dramatic road running through typical limestone country. On either side of the road the hillsides are marked by the escarpment of scars, exposed crags of white, broken rock. The slopes of Ingleborough to the east are lib-

The wild moorland of Garsdale Head. The farms are protected by a screen of trees.

erally dotted with potholes and caves, and the White Scar Caves ★ by the roadside are open to visitors who can walk nearly ¹/₂ mile into the hill. Chapel-le-Dale ★ is the starting point for **Walk 5**. Beyond here two transport systems, separated by nearly 2,000 years, meet. The B6255 runs along an old Roman road, and passes under the Settle and Carlisle Railway next to the famous and majestic Ribblehead ★ viaduct. It is possible to park beyond the railway bridge.

The road now runs across the open moorland of Gayle Moor and Widdale, where unfortunately some sections of the moor have now been covered in the typically dense masses of conifer plantations. Care should be taken to avoid sheep which wander freely over the moor. The road eventually dips down to join the A674 on the edge of Hawes ★ **(B)**. Turn left on the main road, which winds its way along Mossdale. The disused railway that once ran from the Settle and Carlisle line down into Wensleydale can be seen to the left of the road. The Settle and Carlisle itself crosses the road just past the lonely Moorcock Inn. Three-quarters-of-a-mile past the viaduct turn left at **(C)** on to the minor road signposted to Garsdale ★ Station. The road is narrow, hilly, and winding, but gives superb views across the hills that surround Garsdale. It falls steeply downhill and again crosses the railway by Dent Station. One of the problems faced by those trying to make the Settle and Carlisle profitable was always the great distance between the stations and the centres of population: Dent Town ★ is in fact several miles away.

At Cowgill **(D)** turn right and then almost immediately left over the bridge on to the road marked Whernside Centre. The route now follows the river valley down a very narrow and twisting road, past the Whernside Cave and Fell Centre to Dent. This is a delightful spot — a town not a village in spite of its size. The streets are narrow and cobbled, surrounded by stone houses, many of which have been whitewashed. There is a car park on the right-hand side of the road opposite the chapel at the far side of the town. This is the starting point for **Walk 6**. Continue along this road, which now becomes noticeably wider. It crosses the River Dee, follows the river valley, and then swings round to cross the River Rawthey on the way into Sedbergh ★ . It is now a busy market town, and it is difficult to believe that, in the middle of the last century, it was actually less important than Dent. Locals even had to make the journey up till 1863 to vote in elections.

In Sedbergh turn left at the church (E) on to the A684, Kendal road and, after ³/₄ mile, turn left on to the A683 Kirkby Lonsdale ★ road. On the left after ¹/₂ mile is a footpath to the hamlet of Brigflatts, where there is one of the country's oldest Quaker Meeting Houses, built in 1675. It is well worth a visit. The road turns south to follow the valley of the Lune, which marks the western edge of the Dales. The high fells to the left of the road contrast with the more gentle, undulating countryside on the right. Again this route follows that of a Roman road. The road passes through the pleasant grey stone village of Casterton ★ , shortly before reaching Kirkby Lonsdale.

Scale 1:250 000 or ¹/₄INCH to 1 MILE

TOURS

Tour 5
The High Moors

45 miles. Although this tour covers only a comparatively short distance, it takes a surprisingly long time, partly because many of the roads are narrow and winding, but also because there is so much to see along the way. The first part is an exploration of some of the byways of Wensleydale but most of the rest of the trip goes across the wide expanses of moors to the north. Cyclists will find another hilly route, but one comparatively free of traffic.

Leave Hawes ★ on the A684 going east towards Aysgarth ★ and after a mile turn right on to the minor road signposted to Burtersett (**A**). Burtersett is a very tiny but pleasant village. One mile further on you cross a stream and, after that, a broad

track running between stone walls crosses the road. This is the old Roman road to Bainbridge ★ (Virosidum) and features on **Walk 7**. On the approach to Countersett ★, there are fine views over the dale and the broad expanses of Semer Water ★. At Countersett turn left, passing Countersett Hall on the left, and head back downhill to rejoin the A684 at Bainbridge (**B**). The road crosses the River Bain, with its succession of waterfalls, and the small hill on the left just beyond the bridge marks the site of the Roman fort.

After 1½ miles, turn right on to the minor road, signposted to Cubeck, where the road turns sharp left. Thornton Rust ★ is an interesting village, based on a wide main street. Many of the houses are terraced, and barns are also built into the terrace with outside stairways. Continue on this road, which has good views of Wensleydale, until you rejoin the A684, where you turn right. Drive on to Aysgarth

Scale 1:250 000 or ¼INCH to 1 MILE

(C) where you turn left on to the minor road to Carperby ★ . This is a good place to stop for a stroll to see the famous falls and Yore Mill. There is a large car park.

Continue on to Carperby and turn right for Castle Bolton ★ . The castle itself soon appears as a massive feature in the landscape, and it is well worth pausing for a visit. The road turns right at the castle to go down the wide village street. At the next junction, turn left for Grinton ★ and Reeth ★ . The ruins of an old lime kiln can be seen by the still-working quarry and, after that, there are only the wide spaces of the heather-covered moors. On the approach to Grinton, the road passes the picturesque, castellated Grinton Lodge. At Grinton (see also **Tour 6**), turn left on to the B6270 crossing the River Swale to Reeth **(D)**. The houses are rather like those of Bainbridge, clustered round a very large green. There is a suggested stroll here to enjoy the scenery and visit the Swaledale Folk Museum.

Turn right off the B6270 on to the minor road, signposted to Langthwaite ★ . The road takes you up Arkengarthdale following the valley of the Arkle beck to Langthwaite, where there are pleasant riverside strolls. At the end of the village take a right turn marked Barnard Castle ★ , and, in the field to your left, you will see a hexagonal stone building. This is the powder house, where the lead miners stored their gunpowder for blasting. Cross the Arkle beck and turn left on to the road signposted to Eskeleth. This is a narrow, gated road, which gives views across the valley to the old mine workings on the hillside. A large and impressive limekiln stands at the right-hand side of the road.

Tan Hill Inn is the highest, and probably the loneliest, pub in England.

The road then turns very sharply downhill to the left, then turns sharp right over the bridge at Whaw. At the T-junction, turn right on to the road across Arkengarthdale Moor. This is a very remote and lonely stretch of moorland, which marks the northern limit of the National Park as the road briefly leaves Yorkshire and enters Durham, The road passes Tan Hill Inn ★ **(E)**, the highest and surely one of the loneliest in England. Originally, it served local coal miners and the pack-horse trade; today it supplies refreshment to thirsty walkers on the Pennine Way, which runs past its doors.

The road runs down West Stones Dale to the River Swale at Park Bridge, close to Wain Wath Force, upstream of the bridge. Over the bridge, turn left on to the B6270. Keld ★ lies to the left of this road, and is the starting point for **Walk 8**. It is worth making a diversion to the village to see the river gorge and Kisdon Force, as described at the start of **Walk 8**. The main road continues on to Thwaite ★ **(F)** which is a typical close-packed Dales village surrounded by hills, and it is recommended for a stroll. After the village turn right on the minor road signposted to Hawes. This is the famous Butter Tubs Pass, and the Butter Tubs ★ themselves can be seen at the roadside 2 miles up the road. There is a limited amount of parking space. As the road begins to descend, there are spectacular views down into Wensleydale. At the T-junction turn left and immediately right to cross the River Ure and return to Hawes.

Tour 6
Four Dales:
Wensleydale,
Bishopdale,
Langstrothdale,
and Swaledale

54 miles. The four dales covered in this tour each has its own very distinctive character, while the hills between offer some of the wildest moorland in the area. This is very much a rural drive with Leyburn as the only sizeable town on the route. The tour could also begin at Hawes. Cyclists will find this to be a very hilly and demanding ride.

Leave Leyburn ★ on the A684 heading west, signposted to Wensley ★ and Hawes ★. Wensley is the starting point for **Walk 9**, and it is worth pausing to see the church with its elaborate private pews. Continue on the main road, cross the River Ure and look over to your right where you can see Bolton Hall. The road goes through West Witton ★ and, at Swinithwaite ★, you pass handsome Swinithwaite Hall and get a view of the distant walls of Bolton Castle. A mile after Swinithwaite, turn left on to the B6160 signposted to Kettlewell ★. At West Burton ★ **(A)** the road turns right but you can drive straight on up into the village where there is a large green with a curious monument and stocks. It is recommended to stop here for a stroll around the village and to the waterfall.
The main route continues on down the

very narrow valley of Bishopdale. Two-and-a-half miles beyond Newbiggin ★, just after crossing the bridge over the beck, look out on the right for West New House, an outstanding example of a Dales long house with barns and living quarters all under the same roof. It was built in 1635. At the end of the dale, the road climbs up over the moor and then drops down into Cray ★. Just beyond Cray turn right on to the minor road that bends sharply back and is signposted to Hubberholme ★ **(B)**. Turn left at the junction and, at Hubberholme, cross the bridge and immediately right. Hubberholme is the starting point for **Walk 10**.
The road now follows the river to Yockenthwaite ★. Beyond this the road stays close to the river which, with its rocky shelves and grassy banks, is a favourite place for children to paddle. Continue following the signposts to Hawes through Oughtershaw ★ where the road leaves the river to cross the open moorland to Gayle ★ and on to Hawes. Turn right on to the Hawes one-way system **(C)** (see **Tours 4** and **5**), and left on to the minor road to Askrigg ★. Cross the River Ure and turn right on to the very pleasant and peaceful road, signposted to Askrigg. This is suggested as a place to stop for a stroll. It will seem very familiar to followers of the James Herriot television series. In Askrigg take the road to the left **(D)**, signposted to Muker ★ and, where the road forks, keep left. This is a dramatic moorland road, narrow, twisting, and steep, and offering quite outstanding views.
At the T-junction, turn right on to the

The stream of Gunnerside Ghyll winding its way down towards Swaledale.

B6270 (E). After ½ mile, it is worth making a very short detour by turning left towards Ivelet ★ to see the extravagantly arched pack-horse bridge over the Swale. Returning to the main road, continue on down the B6270 down to Gunnerside ★. Swaledale is one of the gentler of the dales, with a broad valley floor, and provides a very pleasant route. At Gunnerside, the road crosses the river and turns right to continue on the opposite bank. This route was known as the Corpse Way, because bodies were carried down the dale for burial at Grinton ★. The Punch Bowl Inn of 1635 at Feetham ★ was a resting place for the pall bearers who carried the bodies in wicker baskets. A mile-and-a-half beyond Feetham, turn right to cross the river on a minor road, signposted to Grinton. This is a delightful little road with views across the Swale. Just before reaching Grinton, the road passes Swale Hall, with its unusual castellated walls. Grinton, which is also visited on **Tour 5**, is dominated by its very fine church. Turn left at the church and immediately right on to the B6270 Richmond ★ road. Two miles out of Grinton, over to the left, you can see the tower and ruined walls of Marrick Priory ★, and a mile beyond that you can see the remains of Ellerton Abbey. At the A6108 (F), turn sharp right to follow the main road, signposted to Leyburn. At castellated Wolburn Hall, the road turns sharp right and then left. After a mile, at the cross-roads, turn right keeping on the A road, and, ¾ mile further on, the road turns sharp left at the junction. Continue on the A6018 back to Leyburn.

Scale 1:250 000 or ¼INCH to 1 MILE

Tour 7
Between the Dales and the Fells, Sedbergh and Kirkby Stephen

47 miles. The tour starts at Sedbergh, but could begin at Kirkby Stephen (B). The route includes two fine market towns, two ruined castles, and a journey among the Cumberland fells that form the western boundary to the Dales National Park. Although main roads are included, cyclists should find them quite comfortable to use.

Leave Sedbergh ★ on the A684, heading west towards Kendal, and, just outside the town where the road forks, take the right fork and continue on the A684. After a mile, you cross the River Lune and then turn right on to the B6257 signposted to Tebay. This is a very pleasant, hilly country lane, bordered by banks and hedgerows instead of the more familiar stone walls. To the right is the valley of the Lune, which marks the boundary of the National Park, and a disused railway. At Waterside Farm, look over to the right where the fine railway viaduct, with brick arches and a central iron span, still stands. Another impressive viaduct can be seen at Beck Foot just before you reach two bridges, one carrying the main-line railway and the other the M6. Passing under the motorway turn right after a mile on to the A685, Penrith road (A). The road follows the line of the motorway to Tebay. Continue on the A685 turning right at the roundabout, signposted to Brough ★ and Kirkby Stephen ★ .

The road now runs through undulating countryside along the Lune valley, with hills rising on either side to Newbiggin-on-Lune ★ . A mile beyond Newbiggin, it is worth a small detour from the main road to Ravenstonedale ★ , which has a most unusual church. Beyond Ravenstonedale. the scenery changes quite dramatically as the road climbs over the heather-covered moorland of Ash Fell. At

The ruins of Pendragon Castle in the Eden valley. Sadly, there are no romantic associations with Uther Pendragon.

98

the foot of the fell, continue on the A685 beyond the junction with the A683, toward Kirkby Stephen ★. This is a pleasant market town at which to pause for a while. The route continues through the town, and you take the third turning on the left, marked B6259 Great Musgrave **(B)**. This pleasant road crosses the Rivers Belah and Eden, after which turn right to Great Musgrave **(C)** and follow the road signposted to Brough. Cross the A66, turn right at the T-junction into Brough, then right at the clock on to the A685 **(D)**, turning back over the A66, then immediately right to Church Brough ★. This is suggested as a place for a stroll. It is an attractive little village, with a picnic area by the river, a Norman church, and a castle.

Return to the A685 and turn right to continue the journey through Brough Sowerby back to Kirkby Stephen. Just past the

church, take the B6259 to Nateby ★, where **Walk 11** starts. The road now continues down the delightful, unspoiled Eden valley. After 3 miles, you reach the ruins of Pendragon Castle ★ **(E)** where you can stop to see the castle and walk by the river. The route turns right at the castle on the minor road signposted to Ravenstonedale and goes across Wharton Fell, which provides magnificent views over the Eden valley. At the A683 **(F)** turn left and follow the main road towards Sedbergh. After 6 miles you pass into the National Park and, just beyond that, is the Cross Keys Inn. You can park nearby for a stroll up the track by the inn to see the spectacular waterfall, Cautley Spout ★, a round trip of a mile-and-a-half. The road now continues along the valley of the River Rawthey between the lowering moorland of Howgill Fells and Baugh Fell, and ends back at Sedbergh.

Tour 8
Barnard Castle and Richmond

40 miles. This is a short tour on the edge of the Dales, which offers a great many places of interest to visit along the way. The countryside tends to be largely undulating farmland, much of it given to crops, unlike the pastures of the sheep farms in the hills. The two principal towns are both of outstanding interest and ample time should be allowed for exploration. Other stopping-off points are also suggested for strolls or for a longer walk. The cycling on this route is easy, but contains busy main road sections.

The tour starts at Barnard Castle ★ by taking the Bowes ★ road from the Market Cross in the centre. The road swings round to the right to cross the bridge across the Tees with the castle on the right-hand side. Across the bridge, turn right and then left on to the A67, which follows the line of a Roman road. Just before Bowes, the road turns under the A66. Turn left (**A**)

and then right into the main street of Bowes. You can park here to visit the castle and this is also the starting point for **Walk 12**. Those who are not stopping, instead of turning right up the main street, should turn left to take the minor road to the A66. Those who have stopped in Bowes need to turn round to join the road up to the A66. At the main road turn right. The main road becomes a dual carriageway, and, after 2 miles on the dual carriageway, turn right at (**B**) on to the minor road signposted to Scargill.

Continue on this road across the River Greta, after which the road bends round to the left; then, almost immediately, take the left turn signposted to Scargill. This pleasantly rural road brings you to Barningham ★ , where stone cottages surround the long, wide green. The road turns left in the village to pass the church and heads back down to the Greta valley. At the T-junction turn left to Greta Bridge ★ , a pleasant spot where you can stop for a stroll. The energetic might like to follow the path up the river bank to the delightful wooded Brignall Banks ★ .

From Greta Bridge, turn right on to the A66 (**C**). After a mile-and-a-half, turn right (**D**) on to the minor road signposted to

Scale 1:250 000 or ¼INCH to 1 MILE

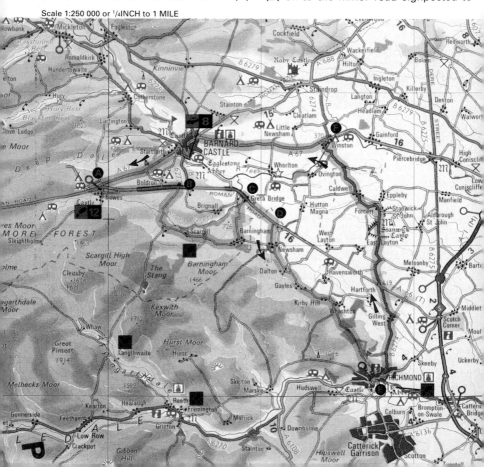

The market square at Richmond. The church in the centre is now a military museum.

Newsham. At the village, turn left, then right and continue on to Dalton, Gayles, and Kirby Hill, which has a large village green and fine views across to the Tees valley. Beyond Kirby Hill turn right at the T-junction and follow this road into Richmond ★ , a town which most definitely requires time to explore. Nearby is Easby ★ where there is a suggested stroll from the abbey along the river bank to Richmond.

Leave Richmond on the A6108 Darlington road and turn almost immediately left at the roundabout **(E)** on to the B6274 signposted to Gilling West and Winton. The road passes the parkland of Aske Hall on the left, and through gentle farmland to Gilling West. The road crosses the A66. After a mile, you can see earthworks in the

fields on the right. They were the defences of Stanwick Camp and were constructed between AD 15 and 17 to enclose an area of 850 acres. This was to be a gathering ground for the forces opposing the Roman invaders but was over-run by the Romans in AD 71. To visit the fort, turn right opposite the gatehouse to Forcett Park, then right again, and the fortifications are on the right.

Back on the main road, continue on past Forcett Park to Caldwell, a village of rich, golden-brown stone houses with bright red pantile roofs. Cross the River Tees to Winton **(F)**. Turn left on to the A67 and return to Barnard Castle.

Tour 9
Fountains Abbey, Fantastic Rocks, and Attractive Market Towns

49 miles. This is a tour which introduces the visitor to the pleasant market towns of Knaresborough, Boroughbridge, and Wetherby, to two great churches — Fountains Abbey and Ripon Cathedral — and to a fine stately home. Between, the scenery varies from dramatic rocky moorland to to the rich agricultural land of the Vale of York. The tour is described starting from Harrogate, but could equally easily be followed from Ripon, Boroughbridge, Knaresborough, or Wetherby. The roads are mostly quiet, though there is always liable to be heavy traffic in and around the towns. Cyclists will find the route hilly, but not too severe.

Scale 1:250 000 or ¼INCH to 1 MILE

Out of Harrogate ★ take the A61 sign-posted to Ripon ★ which leads out past the Exhibition halls. The road passes through Killinghall (A), a typical village of small stone-built houses, and then crosses the River Nidd. At the roundabout (B) turn left to the village of Ripley ★ with its Gothic-styled estate cottages and castle. Continue on through the village and, at the roundabout, turn left on to the B6165. The road follows the edge of Ripley Park, which can be seen more clearly from the top of the hill at Bedlam. Continue on through the village of Burnt Yates, and immediately beyond the village, turn right on to the minor road (C) signposted to Brimham Rocks ★. A mile down the road on the right-hand side is a fine example of a typical old Yorkshire farmhouse with mullioned windows and surrounding stone barns. This is a delightful section of road running between high banks and through woodland. Continue on this road: the road bends sharply left and, after 1 mile, turn right at the crossroads (D). Moorland and rocky outcrops now begin to dominate the scenery. After a mile, you

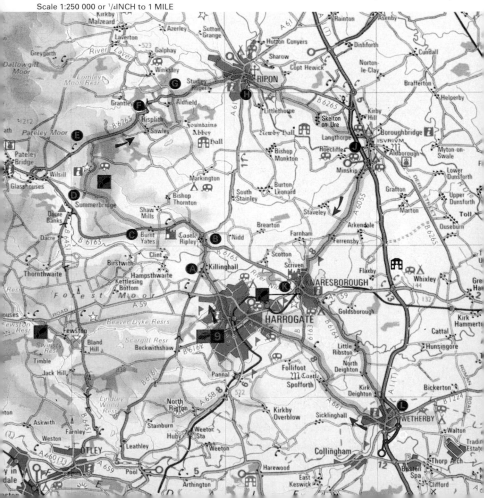

The fantastic shapes created by the natural forces of the weather at Brimham Rocks.

reach the National Trust car park on the left, where you can stop for a stroll round the astonishing rock formations of Brimham Rocks.

From the car park, turn left to resume your journey on the open moorland road. At the junction with the B6265 **(E)** turn right for Ripon. From here there are superb views across the Vale of York to the distant Wolds. After 2 miles, turn right by the Black-a-Moor Inn **(F)** on the minor road signposted to Sawley, a pleasant village with a small green. In the village, turn left into Low Gate Lane, opposite The Sawley Arms. This is a very narrow road which winds along the side of the Skell valley. At the T-junction turn left, and you will see the magnificent tower of Fountains Abbey ★ in the valley below. You can park here at the National Trust car park to visit the abbey or you can continue on the journey to approach the abbey from Studley Roger which will give you a drive through the park and a walk through the water gardens of Studley Royal.

The way continues across the river and back up to the B6265 **(G)** where you turn right for Ripon **(H)**. You pass the turn for the Studley Roger entrance to Fountains Abbey after 2 miles. Ripon is well worth visiting but, to continue the tour, stay on the B6265. It is an easy route to follow: at the cathedral turn right and then left at the roundabout. The waterway to the right of the road is the Ripon Canal, now being restored by enthusiasts — look out for the lock by an old toll house. Ripon racecourse is also alongside the road. Cross the River Ure and, almost immediately, turn at the sign indicating Newby Hall ★ and then left, indicated as Newby Hall and Skelton. The Hall is a splendid seventeenth-century house with formal gardens

reaching down to the river. It is open to the public and is reached by a drive through the park.

The tour is continued by following the main road that turns sharp left towards Boroughbridge. The route passes under the A1 through Langthorpe, and then turns right at the T-junction **(J)** into Boroughbridge. This is a market town that dates back to Norman times, and is centred on the crossing of the River Ure, which is still used by pleasure boats. On the edge of the town are three monoliths, known as The Devil's Arrows. Continue on the B6265 across the river, as it bends first left, then right, but, at the next sharp left bend by the square with the war memorial, leave this road and carry straight on past the Black Bull pub. Turn left at the T-junction and then immediately right on the A6055 for Knaresborough ★ .

This part of the tour passes through gentle agricultural land — a great contrast to the moorland at the beginning. At Knaresborough, turn left at the traffic lights **(K)** on to the A59 York ★ road. This is a town full of character set on a high cliff above the River Nidd and is definitely well worth exploring. Continue up the High Street and, at the traffic lights 1 mile from the centre, turn right on to the B6164 for Wetherby **(L)** along the valley of the Nidd. The route passes through Little Ribston, home of the Ribston Pippin apple. Kirk Deighton is a pleasant village with a majestic church, while Wetherby, like Boroughbridge, is an attractive market town which grew up at the point where the Great North Road crosses the River Wharfe. In the town turn right on the A661 signposted to Harrogate. The road goes through Spofforth ★ , with its ruined castle, and back down a rocky moorland valley to Plumpton Rocks ★ .

The final stage of the tour goes past the Yorkshire Show Ground to Harrogate.

Tour 10
Brontë Country

45 miles. This is a tour on the southern edge of the Dales, which includes visits to Haworth and to other spots that have special associations with the Brontë family. In the end, though, it is not so much the specific locations that create the memories as the area as a whole: the wild moors of Wuthering Heights, the big houses where governesses much like Jane Eyre looked after the children, and the little villages clustered round the tall chimneys of the mills of Shirley. It is also a tour that can be enjoyed for its own sake, regardless of the Brontë connection. The route is not particularly strenuous for cyclists, but includes sections with heavy traffic.

The tour begins at Skipton ★ which is also a stopping place on **Tour 2**. Leave on the A65 Leeds road and continue following this road which turns right at the roundabout just outside the town. The route runs over rough moorland to join Wharfe-dale. At Ilkley ★ , turn right on the road signposted to Ilkley Moor. The road bends left for the town centre. Ignore the next signpost to the moor and turn right immediately past the railway station **(A)**. The road leads off at an angle to bring you up to the edge of the moor. You can park on the right just before the Cow and Calf pub to stroll up to the rocks: the large isolated rock is The Calf; the cliff beyond it The Cow. Continue on this moorland road through Burley Woodhead and, after the second Menston turn, turn right **(B)** for Bingley. After 3 miles, the road bends right and goes downhill: turn left on the road signposted to Micklethwaite. The road bends and twists sharply downhill through the stone houses of the village. The road crosses the canal on a moveable bridge. If you walk down the tow-path to the left for a few hundred yards, you will come to the Bingley Staircase, five interconnected locks that drop the canal 60 feet downhill. At the main road, the A650 **(C)**, turn left — you get a glimpse of the Bingley locks up to your left — and then

Haworth Parsonage, home to the remarkable sisters, Anne, Charlotte, and Emily Brontë.

turn right, past the church, on to the B6429 to Cullingworth **(D)**.

At Cullingworth, turn right on to the B6144, just past The Fleece pub, to Haworth. The road crosses the A629 and gives wide views across the moors above Haworth — which, perversely, is pronounced 'Howarth'. At the A road, cross straight over for the steep descent to the village, and then turn left to cross the railway. Although Haworth is chiefly known for the parsonage and the three famous sisters, it is a place which still preserves a character of its own. It was essentially a mill village in the nineteenth century, a working rather than a romantic place. The Brontës were among the local notables who bought shares in the proposed railway to Keighley, now preserved as the splendid Keighley and Worth Valley Railway, where steam trains still run linking delightful little branch-line stations. The Parsonage has been much altered since the Rev. Patrick Brontë's time, but remains a place of pilgrimage for all admirers of his daughters' works.

The road bends round above the top of the main street of Haworth **(E)** and continues on to Stanbury. This was also a wool village, and you can see stone cottages with long windows on the upper floor where weavers had their looms. This whole area shows the mixture of mills with their tall chimneys and weavers'

cottages: the conflict between mill and handwork formed the basis for Charlotte Brontë's *Shirley*. Stanbury church contains the top section of the three-decker pulpit from which the Reverend Brontë preached in Haworth. There is a footpath on the left at the end of the village to the ruined farmhouse, Top Withins, said to have been the original for 'Wuthering Heights'. Beyond the village near Ponden Reservoir, is Ponden Hall, now a guest house, and the inspiration for Thrushcross Grange.

The road runs over heather moors and, at the signpost to Wycoller Country Park, you can stop to walk to the old weavers' village of Wycoller. Wycoller Hall was the original for 'Ferndean Manor' in *Jane Eyre*. At Laneshaw Bridge, cross the A6068 on a dog-leg and continue up Emmott Lane. Turn right by the Alma Inn and right again at the next junction **(F)**. After 1¾ miles, the road divides: take the right-hand fork to Lothersdale. It was here that Charlotte Brontë worked as a governess in 1839, an unhappy period which led to the writing of *Jane Eyre* **(G)**. Continue on the narrow road to the T-junction, turn left towards Colne, then immediately right up a steep hill, then right again at the T-junction. The road goes across Elslack Moor, with extensive views to Carleton. Go through the village, cross the bridge, and turn left to return to Skipton.

Scale 1:250 000 or ¼INCH to 1 MILE

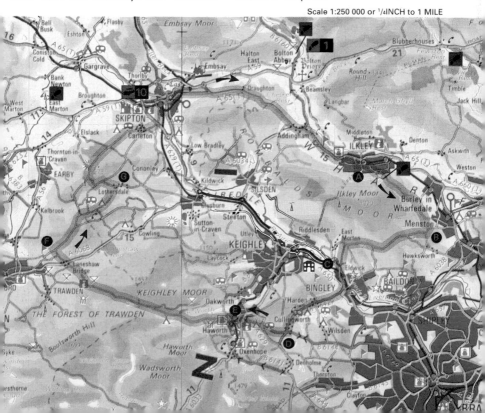

Walks in the Dales

The walks described in this book are all comparatively short, and none goes up to the high moorland. They may be strenuous in parts with a few stiff gradients, but there is nothing that should prove unduly taxing, even to those who do not go walking very often. Nevertheless, it has to be remembered that much of the area consists of rough country, and what may be a gentle stroll on a sunny afternoon can take on a very different character in other circumstances. The following words of caution are not intended to deter anyone from walking in the Dales — far from it — they are intended to help ensure that those who do go walking have a pleasant, rewarding, and above all, safe experience.

The most important elements are climate and weather. A walk which is problem-free in summer can be a very different proposition in winter. Rocks may be covered in ice, and snow can obliterate simple waymarks. Winter walks can be uniquely enjoyable as anyone who has seen the Peaks pristine white, their edges curled over into cornices, can testify. But winter walks on the uplands in snowy conditions are only for those who have some experience and who are properly equipped. Even in summer, however, the weather can play a part. Low cloud can envelope the hills with an effect like fog, and rain driven on a strong wind can chill the body as well as wet it. The answer to these problems is basic and simple, but important.

The first rule is to be prepared for the worst. A three-hour walk may not seem very long but, if it starts to pour with rain and you are on top of a moor without

Opposite and below: *Natural scenery above Clapham; lead mining near Grassington.*

adequate waterproof clothing, the consequences could be serious. If dark clouds start to gather ominously low over your route there is nothing silly about turning back — it is simply common sense. Being lost in cloud on the heights is frightening and potentially dangerous. The golden rule is: if in any doubt about whether to be bold or cautious, opt for caution every time. Walking does not have to be limited to fine, sunny days, provided the walker is properly equipped for the conditions.

The commonest problem that afflicts people out walking is sore feet. Shoes that are perfectly comfortable on city streets may be far less satisfactory on rough and rocky ground — not to mention damp, boggy ground. Wellington boots may keep out the wet, but are often loose fitting and liable to cause blisters. Stout walking shoes or boots will generally make for comfortable — and therefore enjoyable — walking.

The walk descriptions given in this book together with the accompanying maps should ensure that you do not get lost. It is, however, all too easy to decide on a 'short cut' which leads not to an easier route but to some unexpected difficulty. One of the pleasures of walking is finding one's own routes, but this requires good maps. The Ordnance Survey 1:50 000 are excellent and the 1:25 000 even better. And it also requires the ability to read the map when you have it. It is a useful exercise for the beginner to follow someone else's route, but to check it against the map, to compare the marks on the sheet with the reality on the ground.

Many people find that there is no better way to enjoy the Dales than to go walking. It is not necessary to set out with enough equipment for a Himalayan expedition. All that is really needed is the common sense to decide in advance what is actually essential for the safe enjoyment of a walk, and not to settle for less.

Walk 1
Bolton Abbey, The Strid, and Barden Tower

The walk begins at Bolton Abbey, then follows the east bank of the Wharfe up to the torrent of The Strid, and continues on to the romantic ruins of Barden Tower. The return route follows the opposite bank of the river back to the beautiful Augustinian priory. Allow 3 hours for the walk, with extra time for seeing the priory. Please note that the path through Strid Woods is permissive but walkers may use it provided the landowner's consent is not withdrawn.

Start from the car park at **Bolton Abbey** ★ (104) (SE 0754) off the B6160, included in **Tour 1**. The name is slightly odd because the monastic buildings were never an abbey but a priory. Leave the car park by the Village Hall **(A)**, turn right, cross over the main road, and go through the hole in the wall by the sign indicating To The Priory and Stepping Stones. On your left, is a very grand castellated house, which was originally the priory gatehouse, but has had many additions over the years. The more modest, but if anything more attractive, house was originally the Bolton Free School, founded in 1697. But by far the most impressive and beautiful buildings are those of the ancient priory, which you will be visiting at the end of the walk.

Cross the river at the footbridge **(B)** and turn left. Do not follow the obvious path up the steps, but follow the river upstream. The path goes into the woods, dips and climbs, but gradually moves up to the top of the bank, high above the river. At the roadway **(C)** turn left, cross over the stream by the ford and turn left in the direction marked as a footpath. At the river bank, cross the stile by the footpath sign and continue on along the bank.

There is a short cut at the wooden bridge. You can cross the bridge to rejoin the main walk **(E)** for the return to Bolton Abbey. Alternatively, you can drive to this point where there is ample car parking space and join the walk to The Strid and Barden Tower ★. The main walk continues close to the river's edge where there is a chance to watch the large mallard population and the occasional dipper and sandpiper. You may also see the rarer tree-nesting goosander. By the island,

follow the path along the water's edge. Where the path meets the roadway again, cross over the road bridge, and turn left immediately at the end of the bridge. It is encouraging to see, on this walk, how much new tree-planting is going on in this nature conservancy area. There are nesting boxes in the trees to encourage birds to breed here.

As the river narrows and the banks steepen, so the path becomes increasingly narrow and rocky. Keep to the river path to The Strid, a narrow channel between black rocks, through which the river roars. It can look a temptingly narrow gap, but **do not** attempt to jump across. Many people have died over the years trying to do just that, for the river is very deep here with powerful undertows. There is no record of anyone falling in The Strid coming out alive! From The Strid, the easier route to follow is the high-level path; the way beside the river can be awash in a wet season.

At the edge of the woods is an impressive castellated bridge that looks as though it should carry a main road, but is in fact nothing more than a footbridge. It can almost qualify as a folly, because its main function is to beautify the river scene. Continue along the path by the river to beautiful Barden Bridge **(D)**, of uncertain age, but an inscription on the parapet tells you that it was 'repayred' in 1676. Before beginning the return journey to Bolton Abbey, cross the bridge and walk up the road to see the impressive ruins of Barden Tower. The first tower was built in the eleventh century as a stronghold for controlling the surrounding forests, but its present form owes much to the redoubtable Lady Anne Clifford, who paid to have it repaired and improved in 1657. Sadly no one lived here after her time. The Tenth Lord Clifford, known as the 'Shepherd Lord', added the chapel and the priest's house in the fifteenth century and they are still in use, if no longer for their original purpose.

Return to the bridge and turn right down the footpath marked Dales Way. Entering the wood, cross the footbridge and, where the path divides, continue straight on by the riverside. The colour markings seen along the way are for visitors following various nature trails. In general, keep as close as possible to the riverside, following the very clear paths. On the opposite bank, as you approach the gorge of The Strid, the path becomes steep and rocky, passing below small gritstone outcrops. You do, however, get superb views down on to the rushing river. For a while, beyond The Strid, you have a broad, easy path through the woods but, where that path turns away from the river to the right by a bench, continue on the narrower riverside walk. Just as you come to Cowper Gill, the stream that has to be crossed, you will catch a strong whiff of sulphur in the air. It comes from an old sulphur well, once thought to have medicinal uses.

The woods end at the Cavendish Pavilion, where the grassy river banks are a popular picnic area (E). Those taking the short cut rejoin the walk here. Follow the river round to the obvious track up the hillside just before the priory. It brings you to the road and to the extravagant Victorian fountain erected to the memory of Frederick Charles Cavendish (F). At the road turn left, and then left again to visit the priory. The old priory, founded in 1120, is now a beautiful and romantic ruin but, at the Dissolution, the priory church was spared and is still in use. From here take the footpath back to the hole in the wall and return to the start.

Scale 1:25 000 or 2½INCHES to 1 MILE

Walk 2
Malham Cove and
Gordale Scar

This walk starts in the village of Malham and includes visits to what must be the most spectacular natural features in the Dales: Malham Cove with its sheer rock face, topped by a limestone pavement and the awe-inspiring chasm of Gordale Scar. By using the short cut described below, it is possible to make a short walk visiting one or other of the features. Allow 2 hours for the full walk.

The walk begins at the National Park Centre car park **(A)** in **Malham** ★ (98) (SD 9063) which is featured on **Tour 2**. Turn left out of the car park, past the Buck Inn and take the road marked Malham Tarn, Langcliffe ★, Settle ★. A short way up the road, turn right on to the footpath marked Pennine Way. There are special facilities available for taking the disabled on the path to the cove and, by a different route, to Gordale Scar. Information is available at the Park

Centre. As you join the path, look over to your right and you will see, among the stone walls, broad terraces or strip lynchets which are the remains of an ancient field system. The main route will eventually lead uphill along the side of the cove, but it is well worth a short detour along the path to the face of the cliff. The cove is a natural amphitheatre backed by a sheer wall of limestone that rises 230 ft above the valley. At the base of the cliff, the stream of Malham beck gurgles out. Retrace your route and rejoin the path as it heads up a series of steps along the left-hand side of the cove.

At the end of the climb **(B)**, you reach the top of the cove and another strange phenomenon, the limestone pavement. This was once one great slab of rock but, over the millennia, rainwater has eaten into the rock to form deep fissures or grykes. The result is like an oversized crazy-paving. There are also magnificent views, from the distant bulk of Pendle Hill to Rylstone Fell. The walk crosses the limestone pavement along the top of the cove

The dramatic limestone cliffs that frame the deep cleft of Gordale Scar.

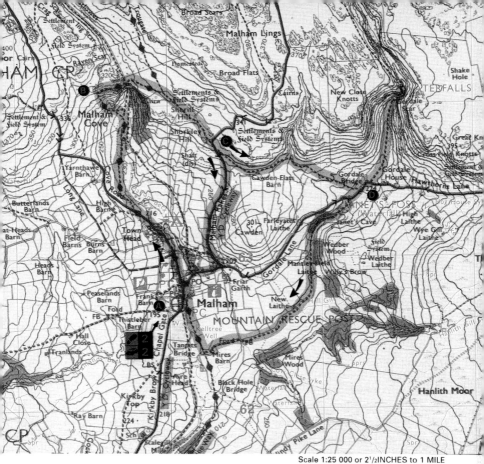

Scale 1:25 000 or 2¹/₂INCHES to 1 MILE

to the stile that leads to a broad, green track, waymarked by yellow dots on posts. Here there is a good view back along the rocky valley of Watlowes. The Pennine Way now turns off to the left, but our path continues straight on, until it reaches a stile on to the road (C). From here you can turn right and follow the road downhill, back to Malham. Alternatively, walkers wishing only to visit Gordale Scar, could simply follow the remainder of the main walk, but in the reverse direction, and then again return on the road.

For the main walk cross straight over the road to the next stile; climb over and follow the signposted path to Gordale that follows the course of the hillside round to the left. As you pass the deep gash on the hillside to your left, Grey Gill, you begin to see very clear strip lynchets, a series of banks and terraces on the hillside, and the path goes through rough stone rings and enclosures. This is an area of settlement that survived over 1,000 years. The rough circles are remains of Iron Age huts, probably begun around 300 BC and surviving through the Roman occupation. The lynchets date from the

Dark Ages and were in use right up to the Norman Conquest.

At Gordale Bridge (D), turn left on to the road and then left again on to the footpath leading up to Gordale Scar. There is only a hint, at first, of the spectacular nature of this chasm, but gradually the high walls close in and the path ends at a series of small waterfalls cascading through a jumble of rocks. Retrace your steps to the road, turn right, cross the bridge, and turn left on to a footpath, signposted Riverside Path Malham. This brings you at once to the impressive waterfall, Janet's Foss. The name comes from a cave by the falls which, according to legend is home to Janet, queen of the fairies. The path follows the stream down a rocky, woody gorge. Here, dippers can often be seen, standing on stones in the stream, eyeing the water for prey, and the lucky walker may catch the electric blue flash of a kingfisher. The path gradually moves away from the river, crossing a broad track on two stiles, and is joined by the Pennine Way coming in from the left. Here the path swings right to return to Malham.

Walk 3
Grassington Moor and the Old Lead Mines

The walk begins in the delightful and very popular town of Grassington and heads straight up the moors to an area where lead has been mined for centuries. The route down from the moors follows a narrow rocky gully to Hebden, and the final leg is an easy stroll along the bank of the River Wharfe, where it follows part of the Dales Way. Allow 3 hours.

The first part of the walk takes you straight up Grassington's ★ (98) (SE 0063) main street, past the town hall and up the road marked No Through Road **(A)**. The road goes steeply uphill, and, if you look over to your left, you can see a pattern of ridges marked out on the hillside. These are the remains of 'Celtic fields', the marks left behind by farmers who were working this land from the time of the Romans to about the seventh century. Near the top of the steep hill, there is a house on the left, Spring Croft, and opposite that a broad track runs off to the right between stone walls. This is the short cut through to Hebden ★ . As the road climbs, so the view opens out over Wharfedale and westward to the prominent hills of Fountains Fell and Pen-y-ghent.

At the top of the hill, you come into an area of mine workings. Among this area of disturbed ground, look out for raised grassy circles, like huge green doughnuts. These are bell pits: a shallow shaft was dug down and the spoil thrown out into a circle around it. The shafts have long since caved in, for some were dug as

long ago as the fourteenth century. There is a very good example on the right of the track opposite a small clump of trees. The metalled road ends by the former mine agent's house and counthouse of Yernbury **(B)**. Turn right along the track marked Bridleway Hebden. This whole area is full of fascinating remains of lead mines: water courses to power machinery and wash the ore, old shafts, spoil heaps, and mine buildings. Up on the moor to the north, you can see a tall stone chimney, with a straight line running down the hillside below it. In the final stage of production, the ore was heated and the lead condensed in the flue — the obvious straight line — before the hot gases finally escaped up the chimney. The track divides **(C)**: one branch goes up towards the chimney; take the other track that bends round to the right. A little further along, beyond a small reservoir, a track leads off to the right to an area of tips, and in here is a mineshaft, now safely covered by a metal grille. It is worth making a short detour to have a look.

Retracing your steps to the main track, continue on as before until a point where the track divides at a signpost saying Bridleway **(D)** and pointing back the way you have just come. Turn left on the wide track that zig-zags downhill. The track comes down to the side of the Hebden Beck where you turn right to follow it downhill. It is a very obvious track which crosses and recrosses the stream. The gorge is very rocky, not limestone but millstone grit; huge square blocks litter the hillside and small outcrops rise up at the edge of the gorge. All the way down there is more evidence of mining, and dams and weirs show where the waters of the beck were once used in the work. At

The remains of old lead mine workings on the moors above Grassington.

Hole Bottom (**E**), cross the stone footbridge and turn left to follow the road downhill to Hebden. The short cut comes in from the right by the first set of houses (**F**). Cross straight over the main road and continue on down the long main street of stone houses overlooking the beck, signposted Burnsall ★ 2¼. At the foot of the hill by the river, turn right on to a footpath marked Grassington Bridge 2 which takes you down to the river bank where you turn right (**G**).

The riverside walk is pleasant, grassy, and tree-shaded, and follows part of the Dales Way. The Wharfe is a broad, fast-flowing river and, beyond it, one looks up to the heather-covered moors. Where the river bends left, and the first houses of Grassington come into view, you cut across the field to the footbridge, and continue on towards the tall building of a former mill by a stream. Cross the stile to join the broad, stony track; then, after crossing the stream, turn left into the field over a stile by a signpost marked Grassington. The path takes you past Linton ★ Falls, part natural and part artificial in the form of weirs. The remains of an old water mill can be seen across the river by the uppermost weir. The path follows the river and then cuts across the field to Grassington Bridge (**H**). Join the road at the bridge and turn right to return to Grassington.

Scale 1:25 000 or 2½INCHES to 1 MILE

Walk 4
Nidderdale

This is a walk at the very top of Nidderdale which starts at Lofthouse and then goes via the dramatically picturesque gorge of How Stean to the delightful, close-packed village of Middlesmoor. From here, the path goes back down to the valley and up the opposite side to the open moorland before the final steep descent to Lofthouse. The walk has a very different character from the other Dales walks, for here the countryside is dominated by dark mill-stone grit instead of the more familiar pale limestone. Allow 3 hours for the walk.

The walk begins at the car park **(A)** by the Institute in **Lofthouse** ★ (99) (SE 1073), a stopping place on **Tour 3**. Before setting out, pause to look at the mellow stone house opposite, with its 1653 date stone above the original, low doorway. Turn left downhill past the Crown Hotel. Turn right at the road. Where the road bends sharply left **(B)** is the point where the short cut returns to the main route. At the next bend **(C)** continue straight on along the road signposted to How Stean Gorge. Continue on, cross the bridge, and follow the road round to the right. The gorge is a famous beauty spot, which you can visit, though a charge is made. The walk follows the road, which continues up the side of the gorge, giving glimpses down to the water bubbling along its narrow passage between tall cliffs. At the point where the road turns left towards the little village of Stean **(D)**, take the footpath to the right signposted Public Footpath Middlesmoor ★, Nidderdale Way. This long-distance path reappears again on the walk. The path crosses the end of the gorge and, at the end of the bridge, continue in

Over the years, the stream has carved strange shapes into the rocks of How Stean Gorge.

the direction indicated by the signpost. Continue following the clearly marked Nidderdale Way to the road **(E)** where you turn left up the steep hill to the village.

Middlesmoor is a beautiful little stone village, the houses closely packed together and joined by a maze of cobbled ways. Turn right down the cobbled lane, between the former Wesleyan chapel and the telephone kiosk to the church. From the churchyard, there is a splendid view back down Nidderdale to Gouthwaite Reservoir ★. From here **(F)** a footpath leads down a flight of steps, which can be taken as the shortest route back to Lofthouse. For the main walk, turn right out of the churchyard gate and follow the broad track round behind the church, which then swings left as a rough track. At the two gates, take the wide farm gate on the right and go straight on through the stile beyond it. Head down via the wooden stile to the wood. Follow the track through the wood, then continue downhill as indicated by yellow waymarkers to the road. At the road turn left **(G)**. Follow the road for ¹/₂ mile. Where the road bends round to the left by a line of conifers, turn right through a gate close to a point where two trees stand, one on each side of the road. Head across the field to the barn by the river.

You have now rejoined the Nidderdale Way, which is marked by yellow arrows. Cross the stile and follow the arrows through the farm buildings. Continue on the obvious track that zig-zags uphill through the trees. At the top of the woods by the farm go through the gate and turn sharp left to follow the waymarked broad track in front of the house. At the next group of farm buildings **(H)**, a broad track comes in from the right; double back to follow this track uphill. Looking back from this point you get a view to the top of Nidderdale, where the valley is blocked by the great dam of Scar House Reservoir ★. The track passes above a conifer plantation and heads for the rim of the valley.

At the top of the hill (**J**) turn right on to the broad track. This is a fine moorland track through wide expanses of heather, busy with the whirr and cackle of grouse. This is typical gritstone country. Go past the curious little hut with a stone tower — a shooting lodge that can almost classify as a folly. Turn right through the gate with the yellow arrow on to the grassy path, and follow the line of the wall to the next gateway. Go through the gate with the arrow. The path swings left to meet the road (**K**). At the road, turn right and go down the steep descent back to Lofthouse.

Walk 5
Ribblehead

This is a gentle walk, with no steep hills and, for much of its length, lies along surfaced paths. Yet it runs between the impressive hills of Ingleborough and Whernside, and offers fascinations of its own including the mighty Ribblehead viaduct and a disappearing river. It starts near Chapel-le-Dale. Allow 1½ hours for the circular walk and 2¼ hours for the full trip.

The walk begins at the Old Hill Inn **(A)** (98) (SD 7477), on the B6255, 4 miles northeast of Ingleton ★ just beyond **Chapel-le-Dale** ★. The pub car park is free to patrons and available for use by non-patrons for a very modest fee. Leave the car park and turn left down the road for approximately 50 yards, then turn right on to the broad

surfaced track **(B)** past the small farmhouse. At first, the walk passes through very gentle country of rich sheep pastures. Soon, however, the ground becomes rougher, with marshy moorland taking over from the grassland. Go past the small conifer plantation and, just before you reach the farm buildings, turn right on to the path marked Broadrake. Then follow the path round as it turns left towards the farm **(C)**. Where you reach the junction with the bridleway that passes in front of the farm **(D)** turn right. The path is now running along the rough lower slopes of Whernside while, across the valley, the view is entirely dominated by the whale-like hump of Ingleborough. Ahead is the Settle and Carlisle Railway with what is correctly known as Batty Moss Viaduct, but is always referred to as Ribblehead.

At the next farm, Ivescar, turn right **(E)**. A little way down the lane, cross over the stile on the left and follow the line of the

Scale 1:25 000 or 2½ INCHES to 1 MILE

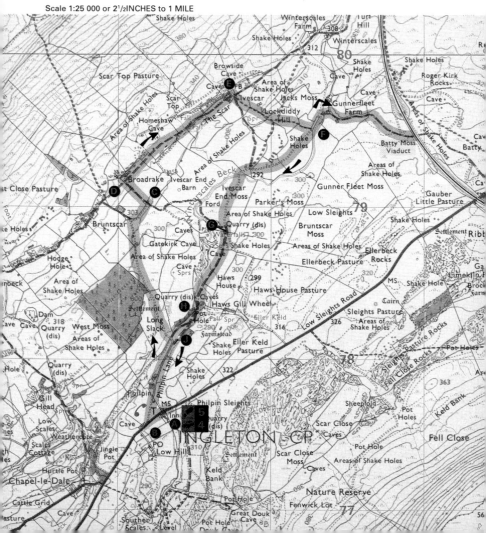

walls down to the farm road to Gunner-fleet Farm **(F)**. Here you can turn right to follow the route to be described in the next paragraph, back to the start. The alternative longer route gives you the chance to see the viaduct close at hand. For the viaduct, turn left, cross the bridge over the stream, and continue on the surfaced track signposted to Ribblehead. As you get close, you can see how the arches are not uniform: Every sixth pier is made more substantial than the rest to give added strength to the structure. The labour involved in construction was immense and arduous, for even in summer, this can be a wild and bleak spot Stone was quarried locally — many of the small quarry remains seen along the walk provided the stone, and, as you reach the viaduct, you can see how massive the stones are, some weighing as much as 8 tons. An army of navvies lived and worked up here for five years, and Batty Green, the shanty town where they lived, once had 2,000 inhabitants. After inspecting the viaduct, return to the farm and continue back to point **(F)**.

Continue down the surfaced track, cross the bridge over Winterscales Beck, and, at the cattle grid **(G)**, leave the roadway and

The very distinctive shape of Ingleborough rising high over the valley.

head diagonally across the field on the right to the gate at the far corner. Continue on down the track, keeping a prominent clump of trees to your left, towards the beck which can be seen carving a miniature gorge down to your right. Head towards a thin line of conifers coming down the hillside, at the lower end of which is a gate and a stile **(H)**. Having reached this point, there is, rather surprisingly, no trace of water. Turn back to your right and you will see the brook disappearing underground. This is a small-scale version of one of the most important features of this area, where the waterways have eaten into the limestone to create caves, pot holes, and a maze of underground rivers. Passing on through the gateway, you continue on down what appears to be a narrow lane between a fence and a wall. This is, in fact, the original stream bed before it performed its vanishing act, as you can see from the smooth limestone blocks underfoot. At the surfaced road **(J)** turn left to retrace your steps back to the main road and across the road to the car park.

Walk 6
Dentdale: Riverside and Fells

This is a circular walk which starts in the picturesque village of Dent. One half of the walk follows a line along the northern flank of the dale, with wide views over the valley, to the surrounding hills. The other half stays almost entirely on the river banks. There is a shorter version which can be comfortably walked in slightly over an hour; alternatively, the indicated short cut can be used as a starting point for the longer, eastern section of the main walk. The whole route should take approximately 3 hours, and is featured on Tour 4.

The village of **Dent** ★ is most easily approached on the minor road from Sedbergh ★, but more spectacular routes are along the moorland road that runs off the A684 at Garsdale Head ★, the route included in **Tour 4**, or on the road from Ingleton ★ via Thornton in Lonsdale.

Whichever way it is approached, Dent appears as a delightful town — for, in spite of its size, it is a town not a village — of narrow, cobbled streets and white-washed, stone houses. The walk starts at the car park at the eastern end of the village street **(A)** (98) (SD 7087) and, from here, a track leads down to the River Dee. Turn left to follow the path, which is part of the Dales Way. The river flows rapidly on its tree-shaded way, stained by the peat of the uplands to a rich, treacly brown. The path briefly joins the road and almost immediately leaves it again at a signpost marked Footpath, Barth Bridge.

At the road bridge **(B)**, cross the river and then head straight uphill on the tree-shaded lane marked Public Footpath to Bankland. At the top of the hill, the path bends round to the right past the back of a traditional Dales farmhouse, and heads across the next field to a group of stone barns. Go through the iron gate by the second stone barn. The path itself is indistinct, but it is easy to see the gaps in walls and hedges — though the exit from the second field is less conspicuous. Look for a stone section in the hedge which

Scale 1:25 000 or 2½ INCHES to 1 MILE

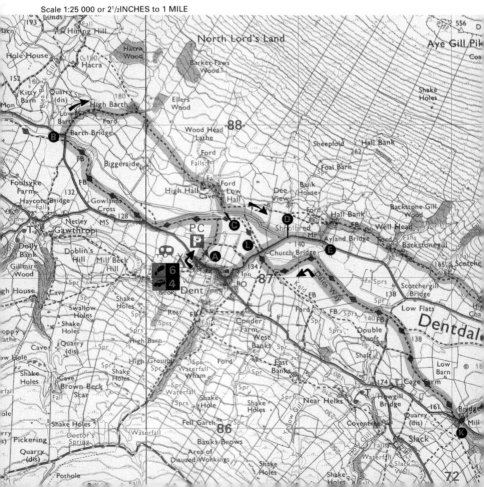

contains the stile. The path brings you to a fine early seventeenth-century building, now used only as a store house for the adjoining kennels. This is High Hall, and its special features are the huge, circular stone chimneys. The path goes through the farmyard. Below Low Hall farm you come to a narrow, metalled road (C). Turn left, and this soon brings you out on to the main Dentdale Road (D). Here you can take a short cut by turning right to cross the river on Church Bridge for the return to Dent. The main walk continues straight on along the main road.

After a couple of hundred yards, turn left (E) by a white milestone, marked S6, up the track to Hall Bank, where it turns right in front of the house and goes through the iron gate next to the stone barn, to the lower of two fields. For the next mile-and-a-half, the path runs parallel to, but above, the road, offering superb views over the dale to the point where it is joined by the side valley carved by Deepdale Beck. Farms turn up with extraordinary frequency, many of them very old — note, for example, the wedding date recorded on the barn by a whitewashed farm, RET

The tight cluster of houses that makes up the little town of Dent.

1681. At the stream, pass through the gate by the side of the farm. You will see a yellow dot on the barn and, beside that, the footbridge. In general the rest of the walk is waymarked by yellow dots and arrows. At the track with the concreted path, the walk passes between the farm buildings. At the end of this section, you meet a roughly surfaced car track which leads back downhill through the cluster of buildings of Bankland. At the road (F), turn left. After 300 yards turn right on to the footpath signposted to Lovers' Leap opposite the large house, Basil Busk (G). The path leads down to a footbridge (H) over the river, from which you can look down on the river bubbling through a narrow, rocky gap — the Lovers' Leap itself. Do not, however, cross the bridge, but turn right to follow the path beside the river. You are now once again on the Dales Way, which will be followed all the way back to Dent.

The river here is much more turbulent than it was at the beginning of the walk, because its waters are constantly swelled by streams running down from the hillside. The meadows alongside the river are lush and, in summer, bright with flowers. At the next footbridge, cross the river and turn right past the ford (J) to follow the path. At the second wall do not use the gate but pass through the stile with the yellow waymark. The path now turns diagonally uphill, away from the river, to Mill Bridge (K). Cross over the bridge, and turn right on to the footpath marked Church Bridge. Follow this path down the side of Deepdale beck until it joins the River Dee, then continue following the riverside path all the way to Church Bridge (L). At the bridge turn left to follow the road up to Dent, and continue on this road. It goes past the church, which is impressively large, and also passes a huge stone slab commemorating a native son, Adam Sedgwick, who was a pioneer geologist at Cambridge. The cobbled street bends round to the right to bring you back to the car park.

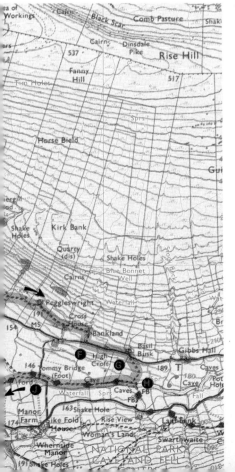

Walk 7
Semer Water and
the Roman Road

This walk starts at the north end of Semer Water, then climbs up a craggy hillside before dropping down the track of the old Roman road to the attractive Wensleydale village of Bainbridge. The final stage leads back up the often dramatic valley of the River Bain. Two shortened versions are possible, missing out either the riverside walk or the Roman road. Allow 3 hours for the full walk.

The walk begins in the car parking area at the end of **Semer Water** ★ (98) (SD9287) on **Tour 5** which is reached by taking the turning to Countersett ★ off the A684 at Bainbridge ★. At Countersett turn sharp left down the steep hill and cross the bridge to the parking area **(A)**. Semer Water is very popular with dinghy sailors

The unmistakable straight line of the Roman road across the moors above Bainbridge.

and windsurfers, and, on fine weekends, can become quite crowded. It has a beautiful setting with the hills rising steeply all around it, and woods creeping right down to the water's edge. From **A**, walk across the three-arched stone bridge over the River Bain which drains away from the lake. Immediately past the bridge, turn left through a gate on to a footpath signposted Marsett Lane **(B)**. The first section of the path leads through the pleasant lakeside woodland, and then gradually heads away from the lake, rising steadily uphill. The path ends at a stile in the corner of a field. Cross the stile to join the

road, turning left to continue in the same general direction. The road turns downhill and, at the bottom of the dip, almost opposite the tip of Semer Water, there is a barn in a field, and a signpost by a gate saying Footpath Countersett and Crag Side Road **(C)**. Go through the gate and cross the simple flagstone bridge over the stream; go through the gate with a yellow arrow alongside. Climb the steep, grassy hillside heading on a diagonal for the far corner of the field. Yellow markers show the position of stiles in the walls and lead you on until you join the tarmac road at a right-angled bend **(D)**. Join the road and continue straight on in the direction you were heading. Up to your left, the hilltop is topped by a line of crags and scarred by the tumbled stone blocks of an old quarry. From here there is a splendid view back over Semer Water. Follow the road as it swings round below the crags for $^3/_4$ mile until it is crossed by a broad, straight, stony track running between stone walls **(E)**. Turn right on to this track.

You are now walking on the Old Cam High Road, built over the moors from the fort of Virosidum down in the valley at Bainbridge. It has the typical straight line favoured by the Romans, but you can also still see how it is built up above the surrounding land. This is a lovely, lonely stretch of countryside, where there is little to disturb the peace apart from the cry of curlew winging up from Semer Water, and it offers a superb view up and down the length of Wensleydale.

At the end of the track **(F)**, turn left to continue downhill to Bainbridge. Those who want to take the shorter route should turn right and walk back up the hill to Countersett, past Countersett Hall, home of the Quaker Richard Robinson who lived there in the seventeenth century. The main walk now goes past a splendid example of Dales enclosures, a group of quite small fields, divided off by stone walls and each one containing its own field barn. The source of building stone can be seen in the line of crags on the brow of the hill. The road ends at Bainbridge **(G)**, a village of contrasts. There is a very large village green around which the buildings are clustered together, in tight groupings of houses and barns, and the two most imposing buildings seen on the walk are the Temperance Hall of 1910 and The Rose and Crown down by the green. Where the road divides, turn right in the direction indicated as Aysgarth ★ and Leyburn ★ and, at the main road, turn right. Cross over the bridge where the River Bain tumbles in a series of water-

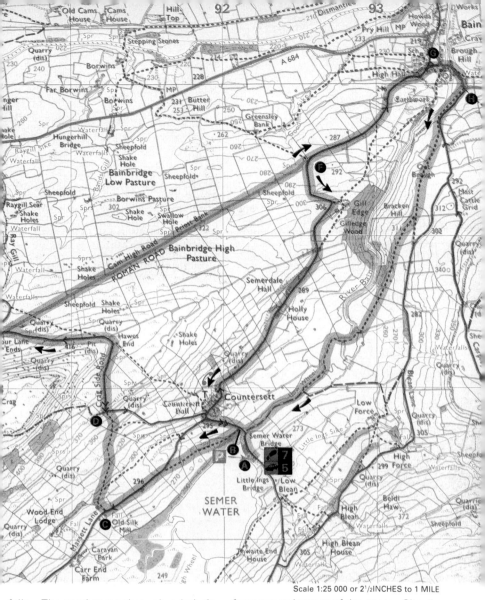

Scale 1:25 000 or 2½ INCHES to 1 MILE

falls. The road turns through a hairpin bend **(H)** and, at the apex of the bend, turn right on to the footpath signposted to Semer Water.

The path Is well marked by yellow way signs and signposts. The only point that needs special attention is at the wall with two stiles, when you should go through the stile on the right. At first, the path follows a high-level route up the side of the river gorge. The Bain is continually fed by small hill streams and, especially after rain, it boils and thrashes over the rocks in a very spectacular fashion. There is a particularly attractive stretch half-way along the route, where the opposite bank is densely wooded, with trees reaching

from top to bottom of the gorge. Shortly after that, the path turns downhill to join the river bank. Now the river is altogether tamer as it meanders in extravagant curves through the meadows and fields, its banks bright with flowers, while reeds and lilies grow in the still water at the river's edge. The riverside walk ends at the bridge.

Those who want to try the second alternative short walk should follow the road up to Countersett village from the bridge, and then either continue on the road down to Bainbridge, to join the main walk or turn right off the road on to a footpath marked Gill Edge which also leads down to Bainbridge.

121

Walk 8
Keld and the Swale Valley

This circular walk starts at Keld and follows the valley of the Swale to Muker and back again. Although the two halves of the walk follow very similar lines, they have very different characters. The route south is along a high-level path, part of the Pennine Way, while most of the return route is a pleasant stroll on grassy river banks. It should be noted that this section of the Pennine Way is very rocky and walkers need to be properly shod. The alternative route offered is not much shorter in miles, but offers much easier walking. Allow 2¹/₂ to 3 hours for the full walk (5 miles).

The Swale winds its way down through the rocks near the village of Keld.

Keld (91) (NY 8901) is on **Tour 5**. It lies just off the B6270 between Thwaite ★ and Kirkby Stephen ★. The walk itself starts at the bottom of the village by the sign saying Public Footpath to Muker ★ **(A)**. The path runs out past the village graveyard into woodland, where it divides **(B)**. Ignore the path going downhill and continue on the route signposted Pennine Way. The view down on to the river is quite magnificent. There is a brief glimpse of the waterfall, Kisdon Force, on a tributary stream, while the river itself has carved a deep gorge between tall, limestone cliffs, reminiscent of Dovedale in Derbyshire. A little further on the path divides **(C)** beneath a small crag. The main walk continues to follow the Pennine Way to the right, but from here you can take the option of an easier route by taking the left-hand track downhill to the valley. Those who opt for the short cut will find an easy-to-follow track by the river, and there is no difficulty about picking up the main route again as the two converge near the only footbridge across the Swale downstream from here.

The main route is very rough and stony, and, for the first part, the view of the valley is closed off by the trees that cling to the precipitous slope below. Then the woodland ends and you look out over to the disused lead mines that surround the stone buildings of curiously named Crackpot Hall. The deep cleft of Swinner Gill bites deep into the hillside, cut by another tributary stream adding its waters to those of the Swale. The river valley itself has now broadened out and the river far below appears as a glistening line threading through bright green fields. Gradually the view opens up: the river swings round to the east, the valley becomes ever broader, and the surrounding hills lose their hard, craggy edges to become softer and rounder. The effect is felt on the walk, as the hard, rocky path gives way to a green track that begins to lead steadily downhill. Looking back from this point, there is a fine view straight up Swinner Gill.

At the signpost where the Pennine Way swings sharply off to the right **(D)**, continue straight on, heading down towards the village of Muker. You get a very good view of the village, and you can see how it developed as a close-packed knot of houses in the broad, flat area formed where Straw beck and the Swale meet. At the bottom of the hill, the track turns through a hairpin bend and heads off to the village about 100 yards away. Only a small diversion is needed to explore this attractive village. The way, however, turns left down a tree-shaded lane **(E)**. At the far side of the field entered by a gate, marked Single File, Meadowland, there is a stone barn close by the river. At this point **(F)** the short cut rejoins the main walk, which now doubles back to the footbridge.

Cross the river and, on the far side of the bridge, turn left along the path indicated by the signpost as leading to Keld **(G)**. The next section of the walk lies along the flat, green river bank. The scenes are not as dramatic as those from the Pennine Way, but there is no shortage of wildlife to look out for: in summer, swallows and the occasional heron can be seen, while rabbits are found in profusion, and there is a good chance of seeing the rabbit's arch enemy, the stoat. As the path nears Swinner Gill, it turns away from the river and begins an uphill climb. The gill itself is crossed by a footbridge below a series of small waterfalls, after which the steady climb continues. At the top of the hill, a whole new vista opens up, with views of the moorland to the north. The path then crosses above a steep, rock-strewn slope created by spoil from the old lead mines.

Beyond that is another fine view of the limestone gorge glimpsed at the start of the walk. A bridge crosses the path over Kisdon Force. A signpost indicates the Pennine Way continuing straight on, but this walk turns left down by the side of the waterfall **(H)**. Cross the footbridge over the river and turn right up the steep path which brings you back on to the original path out of Keld. Turn right to return to the village.

Scale 1:25 000 or 2½INCHES to 1 MILE

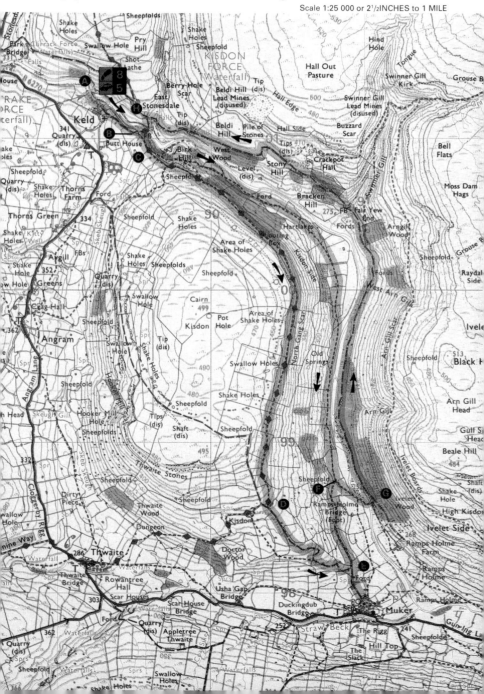

Walk 9
Wensley, Redmire, and Bolton Hall

This is a very different type of walk from the other Dales routes for, instead of the natural beauties of rough countryside, it lies for much of the way through the artificially created beauties of a country house estate. There is, however, no shortage of natural attractions, with wide views across Wensleydale, and two markedly contrasting villages, Wensley and Redmire. Allow 3 hours.

Wensley ★ (99) (SE 0989) is on **Tour 6**. It lies on the A684 just over a mile west of Leyburn ★ . There is room to park in the area close to the church.

The walk starts at the entrance **(A)** to Bolton Hall. Pass the lodge, go through the gates, and head straight up the main driveway. On either side is grassland, dotted with massive, mature trees. At the picturesque little building, Middle Lodge, the driveway passes through an avenue of trees. Over to the left you can glimpse a handsome, elliptically arched stone bridge across the River Ure. This is Lords Bridge, which carries another of the avenues that run up to the main hall. Everything surrounding the hall has its touch of grandeur: even a little bridge over a tiny stream has an ornate balustrade.

The avenue passes in front of Bolton Hall **(B)** originally built in 1678, but rebuilt in 1902 following a fire. It remains, however, a handsome house, with a balustraded parapet and a very large phoenix weather vane. It faces out across the valley with fine views across to the hills of Melmerby Moor. Immediately beyond the house are a pair of wrought-iron gates, topped with crowns and dated 1930, and here there is a crossing of avenues, but continue straight on along the broad track that skirts the woodland at first and then passes through into the trees. These woods are used for rearing gamebirds which can be seen in profusion, strutting quite nonchalantly along the path. Notice the numerous vermin traps set at the edge of the woods. Where the dense, fenced-off woodland gives way to more spacious mixed woods, the air becomes loud with the hooting of wood pigeons, and rabbits can be seen playing among the wayside flowers. The mixed woodland contains some massive old, gnarled oak trees and tall beech. This leads to one

of the most beautiful stretches of the walk, where the ground to the left slopes steeply away to the wandering River Ure, the bank dominated by beech and oak.

Emerging from the wood, there is a distant view of the ramparts of Bolton Castle. Two hundred yards beyond Wood End farm, a footpath leads away to the right, turning back at a sharp angle **(C)**. This offers a short cut, which can be followed across the railway line to rejoin the main walk at the road. Nearing Redmire ★ is the tiny church of St Mary, its graveyard kept neat and trim by grazing sheep. It is a very plain twelfth-century church, entered through a typical Norman doorway, with a chevron pattern on the arch. Inside is a Norman font, but the only obvious decorative features are the gilded roof bosses. Leave the church and continue on to the village of Redmire turning right at the road **(D)**. It is a village of great charm, with farms and cottages scattered round the green, which boasts a tall, wide-spreading, ancient oak tree. Those who have already worked up a thirst can call at either The King's Arms or The Bolton Arms. At the end of the green, almost opposite the road sign to Leyburn,

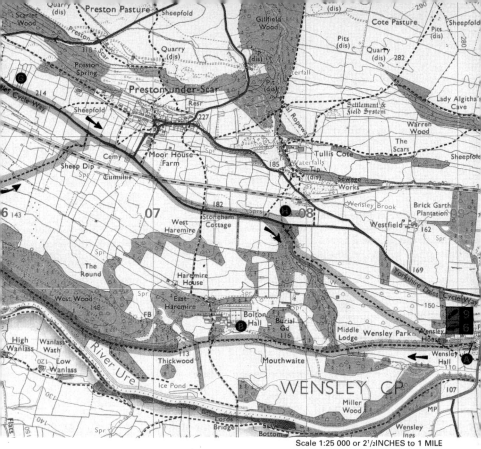

Scale 1:25 000 or 2¹/₂INCHES to 1 MILE

turn right on to a lane between two houses **(E)**. The footpath is not very distinct but the stiles and gates in the field boundaries are easily spotted. At the little stream, turn left to follow the wall back up to the road by the footpath sign. At the road, turn right and then, almost immediately, turn off up the driveway marked Elm House **(F)**. Once through the gateway, take the route marked Elm Woods to the left. At the wooden chalets, turn right through the wall at the stile marked by a yellow arrow. Looking over to your left, in summer, you can see a line of brilliant foxgloves marking the railway. In one field there is a stile in front of a barn on the opposite side of the railway, giving access to the line. Use the farm gate to the left of the stile. Cross the line. Head diagonally across the field, passing above the stone barn. From here you get fine views back to Bolton Castle and along the dale, back to the hills around Hawes ★. At the roadway **(G)**, turn right and continue along the road for a mile-and-a-half.

From the road, the view to the south is across Wensleydale, while that to the north is closed off by the escarpment of the hill. At first, bare rock tops the hill, but the harsh lines are soon softened by woodland. After ¹/₄ mile, a track joins the road from the right, bringing the short cut back to the main walk. The village of Preston-under-Scar spreads out in a long line beneath the crest. Everywhere there are signs of mines and quarries and a tall chimney pokes out above the trees to the east of the village. This road is part of the Yorkshire Dales Cycle Way.

Cross over the railway line, pass a small quarry and Stoneham Cottage, and you come to a patch of woodland on the right. Near the end of these woods, turn right on to a wide track through a gateway marked by a yellow arrow **(H)**. The route is not the obvious wide track through the woods, but, 50 yards from the gate, take the grass track leading off to the left towards a gate into a field. Bear right through the gate and go round the field keeping to the edge of the wood. Cross over the rough ground to the open parkland. The path can be seen as a faint track across the field. Head off diagonally from the little stone cottage towards a large solitary oak tree, beyond which is the point where woodland comes to meet the fenced drive. At the gate, turn left into the drive and return to Wensley.

Walk 10
Hubberholme and
Langstrothdale

The walk starts in the picturesque hamlet of Hubberholme. The first part of the walk lies along the bank of the Wharfe, then turns back to climb steeply up the hill and follow a line along the limestone scar above Langstrothdale to the rocky gorge of Cray Gill. From the end of the gill there is a short stroll back to Hubberholme. Two shorter alternatives are available: the footpath from Hubberholme to Scar House divides the walk into two roughly equal parts. Either start by climbing up the path to Scar House (E) to join the main walk by turning right at the top of the hill, or follow the first part of the walk through Yockenthwaite, and then descend from Scar House. Allow 2½ hours for the main walk, 1½ hours each for the short versions.

Hubberholme ★ (98) (SD 9278) is a hamlet off the B6160, 4 miles north of Kettlewell ★ . Take the turning to the left, ³⁄₄ mile north of Buckden. There is car parking on the river bank by the church (A). This is a delightful spot, with the busy river gur-

Scale 1:25 000 or 2½INCHES to 1 MILE

gling under and old stone bridge, overlooked by the ancient inn. The George Inn is the setting each New Year's Day for the 'Hubberholme Parliament'. It was once the vicarage which is why the annual land lettings are held here as they have been for 1,000 years. Take the path past the church, signposted Footpath to Scar House and Yockenthwaite ★ Dales Way. It is well worth pausing for a few minutes to see the ancient church. It is famous for its rood screen, rood loft, and modern carved pews. Where the path divides (**B**) take the direction indicated as Yockenthwaite Dales Way, which follows the river bank. The broad track leading uphill provides the link for the two short walks. Those intending to take the short eastern route, should turn up this track and rejoin the main walk at (**E**). The main walk stays quite close to the River Wharfe which, in dry weather, is a placid stream much favoured by paddling children, but, in the rain, becomes a chocolate-brown torrent. In medieval times, the inhabitants of Langstrothdale carried corpses down the valley to Buckden, then over the hills on the 'Corpse Way' to Arncliffe for burial. Once, when the river was in flood, the body was carried away by the waters. Modern walkers should not experience similar problems! The hamlet of Yockenthwaite appears as no more than a scat-

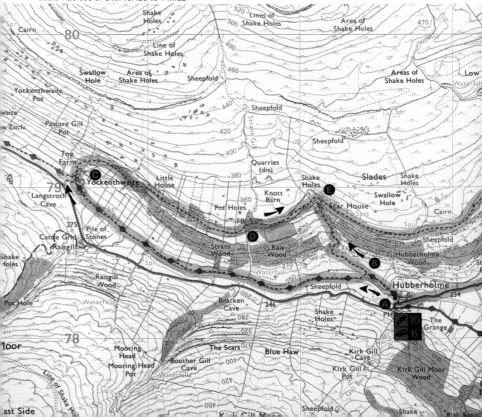

tering of traditional stone houses and barns. It is, however, an ancient settlement with a Norse-Celtic name meaning 'Egon's clearing'. Settlement, however, must go back even further, and those with a keen interest in archaeology and ancient history might care to continue along the north bank of the river past the high-arched pack-horse bridge, for just under ¹/₂ mile when they will come to the Yockenthwaite stone circle. It consists of an almost perfectly circular ring of twenty stones. This was first built in the Bronze Age, perhaps as long ago as 2000 BC. After viewing the stones, return to Yockenthwaite.

The route for the walk itself now continues as follows. At the farm buildings (C) just before the road bridge, cross the stile on the right marked with a yellow dot, and pass in front of the imposing farm buildings with the wrought-iron gate. At the end of the farm buildings, look for a signpost and follow the rough track pointing up hill indicated to Cray ★ and Hubberholme. The track swings round as it climbs steeply in a semicircle. At the top of the hill, turn right over the stile by the footpath sign.

The next stage of the walk follows the rim of the valley, and is waymarked by orange blobs on boulders and walls. A word of caution: be careful not to mistake

bright patches of yellow lichen for way marks. At a point opposite the deep wooded gill on the opposite side of the valley, look out for a signpost and follow the well-worn path indicated that leads through the trees. At the edge of the wood, the path turns slightly to the right to follow the wall at the edge of the steep slope. From here, there are wide views down the valley. This is a very rocky landscape with the edge of the escarpment marked by a limestone pavement, a small-scale version of the more famous pavement above Malham ★ Cove. Farmers have incorporated quite massive boulders into walls and buildings. When you reach a small woodland that seems to block your way (D), turn uphill and you will see the yellow marker indicating the footbridge. This leads over a jumble of massive boulders above a deep pothole. This provides entry to the cave system, but can only be explored by experienced and properly equipped cavers. Beyond the wood, the walk changes character as it opens out on to pleasant grassland. At Scar House (E) the way divides. The short cut is the track leading steeply downhill; the route to Cray continues straight on. Below the hilltop cairn, the walk follows a broad grassy platform from which there are wonderful views. The river, far below, bends sharply to the south, so that the walker can see straight down Wharfedale. The path now turns slightly uphill to follow the same general line but passing above the low stone scarp. At the approach to the deep gully, the path swings round to the left — again look out for yellow marks on boulders — and, looking down into the gully, you will see the footbridge. Cross the bridge and turn slightly to the right to follow the path between a wall on your left and the stream on the right. By the barn, pass through a gate marked Meadowland, Single File and head downhill.

As you approach the bottom of the valley, you get a good view of the waterfall above Cray High Bridge. At the farm buildings (F), you will see the signpost down to the right where the path divides. Turn sharp right in the direction indicated, down the footpath signposted to Stubbing Bridge, down a narrow lane between stone walls in front of the farmhouse. The footpath heads downhill following the curve of the hillside to the bank of Cray Gill. The little river rushes downhill over a series of rock ledges that create waterfalls and rapids in this delightful wooded gorge. At the road (G) turn right to return to Hubberholme.

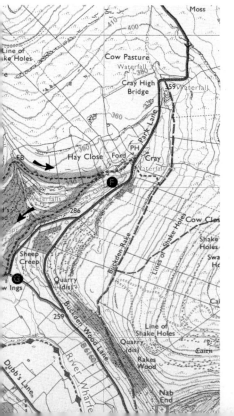

Walk 11
Nateby

This can be made into one continuous walk, but is really two distinct, short walks of very different character, one to the south and one to the north of Nateby. The more southerly walk includes a stroll down by the River Eden and a close view of a magnificent medieval hall. The more northerly route starts in gentle country lanes but eventually reaches to the foot of the fells before returning to the village in the valley. Allow 1¹/₂ hours for each walk.

The walks are featured on **Tour 7**, and both start in the centre of the village of **Nateby** ★ (91) (NY 7706) which lies on the B6259 1 mile south of Kirkby Stephen ★. The actual starting point is the junction of the B6259 with the B6270 **(A)**.

For the first, walk a few yards back from the junction towards Kirkby Stephen. At the village shop, turn left up the footpath marked Bridle Way to Wharton. The path runs between two fences and then crosses a rocky field to reach the River Eden. Follow the river bank round to the left and then cross the river on the footbridge **(B)**. Turn left and cross the field to the barns by the surfaced farm drive. Follow the drive on into the farmyard behind Wharton Hall **(C)**. This magnificent building was begun in the fourteenth century, and extended over the next 100 years. Part of it is still in use, but the rest is a picturesque ruin. The

At the end of the day, tired walkers will find plenty of hotels and pubs in Kirkby Stephen.

noble gatehouse with the Wharton coat-of-arms now leads only to an empty court-yard. The whole group, however, remains most impressive. The walk passes very close by, but it must be remembered that this is a private house. Do not walk past the gatehouse, but turn through the farm gate on the right and follow the track that swings round to the left, past a three-gabled wooden barn. Over on the left, on the far side of the river, you can see broad terraces on the hillside, these are strip lynchets, used for crop growing by medieval farmers.

The path now swings away from the river to head up to the farm, Low Houses. Continue on past the farm and join the road **(D)**. Turn right on to the road. Beyond the road is one of the bridges on the Settle and Carlisle Railway. After a few hundred yards, you come to a very fine seventeenth-century house with a date plaque over the door bearing the inscription: 'Lord give me leave I may go in when I come forth free from all ills. This house was begun 1661' **(E)**. It is a typical farm house of the period with barns and living quarters all under one roof. Turn right here, past the telephone box, down the green lane running between stone walls. At the end of the lane, continue on, keeping the stone wall on your right-hand side, and head for the little knoll with a clump of trees on top. From here, there are fine views of the surrounding fells, and you can also see the full extent of Wharton Hall. The path leads you down to the driveway to the Hall. Continue straight on across the field to retrace your steps back over the footbridge and return to Nateby.

The second walk has the same starting point **(A)**. Again walk a little way up the Kirkby Stephen road, then turn right, opposite the Methodist chapel. At the bottom of the short hill, cross the beck on one of the neat stone bridges and turn left up the lane past the farm buildings. By the ford **(F)**, turn right up the track. The path crosses a stone bridge over a disused railway, and it is interesting to look down the cutting to see how effectively nature is taking over, as trees and shrubs colonise the old line. The path now heads downhill on a narrow, tree-shaded bridle-way. Shortly after crossing a wooden footbridge over a stream, the way divides **(G)**. Take neither of the obvious paths, but instead turn right through the farm gate into the field, and cross it to find the railway bridge approximately 100 yards to the left of the small brick building.

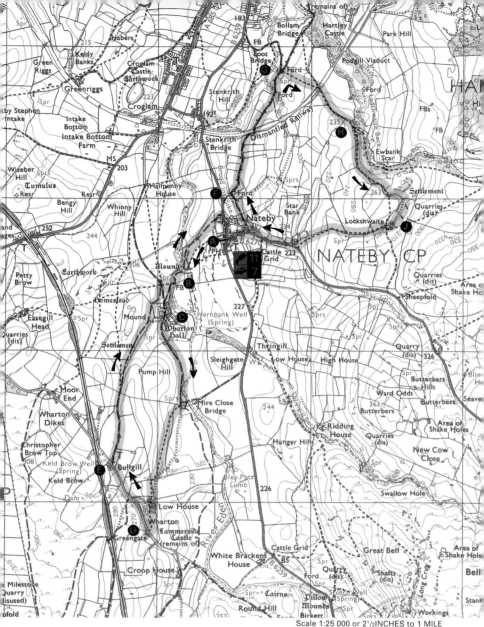

Follow the path, keeping the wall on your left-hand side, straight up the hill. Cross the stile and continue up the green lane. Looking back from here you get a fine view of the fells and of the handsome railway viaduct across Ladthwaite beck.

At the end of the lane (**H**) by a small stone barn, turn left through the gate to follow the track as it heads round the rim of the deep valley cut by Ladthwaite beck. Where the valley swings to the left, you can see the cliffs of Ewbank Scar. From here there is a panoramic view of the Cumbrian hills. Continue following the deep rutted track as it goes through a patch of woodland and turn right beyond a stile marked with a white arrow. Follow the track round behind the farm buildings (**J**). Go into the farmyard and take the gate to the left. Do not follow the obvious farm track but keep close to the wall on the left. This is known locally as The Old Postman's Track. At the point where you see a hedgerow apparently barring your way, look out for a stile in the wall; pass through it and continue downhill to join the road by the farm. At the road turn right to return to Nateby.

Walk 12
Bowes and the Greta Valley

The first part of this walk takes you on a lonely moorland road; the second follows the line of the River Greta as it winds its way down a rocky gorge. A large section of the walk follows the long-distance footpath, the Pennine Way. Allow 3¹/₂ hours.

Bowes ★ lies just south of the A66, by the junction with the A67 from Barnard Castle ★ and is featured on **Tour 8**. The actual walk does not include the main street, but it is worth walking to the western end of the town to see the ruined castle and, just beyond that, Dotheboys Hall, made famous by Charles Dickens in *Nicholas Nickleby*. The walk begins at the eastern end of the main street (**A**) (92) (NY 9913). The link road from the A66-A67 junction leads down from the north, and the walk goes on the continuation of this road to the south, signposted Gilmonby ¹/₄ mile. Cross the wooded valley of the Greta on the narrow stone road bridge and continue to follow the road to Gilmonby, a hamlet of neat little stone cottages. Where the road divides, continue on round to the right in the direction signposted to Sleightholme (**B**). The walk now continues on this road for 3 miles. From the top of the first hill, you can look across to your right and see Bowes Castle in its commanding position above the Greta valley. The road soon brings you out on to the lower slopes of Gilmonby Moor. There is a short section which passes through a fine mixed woodland of mature trees, but beyond that there is just the open moor. In parts it is covered in a blanket of heather, while other parts are marshy and boggy. The road has an air of great remoteness, with little to disturb the peace, apart from the gurgle of moorland streams and the harsh calls of the grouse on the heather moors.

The road comes downhill, off the moor, to join Sleightholme Beck. Just beyond the farm buildings, there is a cattle grid and, beyond that by the road sign, there is a small signpost by a gate on the right-hand side of the road, saying Pennine Way (**C**). Go through the gate and turn back in the direction indicated by the signpost towards the low crags on the opposite bank of the beck. Cross the footbridge over the beck, to the right of the crags. Across the bridge, turn right and continue

to follow the line of the beck on the path that keeps to the higher ground above water. As the river bends away to the right, look for a gate in the stone wall at the top of the bank, with a white sign saying Pennine Way (**D**). Turn right through the gate and follow the peaty track alongside the stone wall. At the building Trough Heads, the Pennine Way turns away to the left. Do not turn this way, but keep straight on following the narrow track beside the stone wall. Follow the line of this wall as it turns left at the edge of the woodland, still following

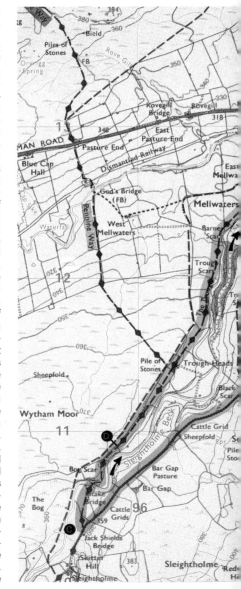

the line of the beck which is now flowing through a deep, rocky gorge. Continue along the path downhill, heading for the farm buildings of East Mellwaters (**E**). Follow the track round the farm, on the side away from the river and, at the edge of a farmyard, you will see a yellow arrow and, in white paint, the letters PW for Pennine Way. Turn left as indicated by the arrow. Head straight across the field to the point where the trees come down to the beck; cross the beck on the footbridge (**F**). Turn left over the footbridge and head for the gate by the stone barn. Turn right

past the farm, go through the gate beside the farmhouse, and left on to the track indicated by the Pennine Way signpost.

This broad track follows the line of the River Greta, while the bold outline of Bowes Castle makes a prominent landmark up ahead. The Greta valley is wider and less dramatic than that of Sleightholme Beck, but is still extremely attractive and varied. The way now runs on a broad metalled track past a number of farm houses to the village of Gilmonby. At the road (**G**), turn left and return to Bowes.

Scale 1:25 000 or 2½INCHES to 1 MILE

CONVENTIONAL SIGNS
1:250 000 or 1 INCH to 4 MILES

ROADS
Not necessarily rights of way

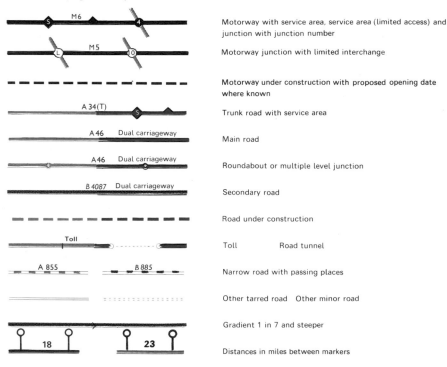

Motorway with service area, service area (limited access) and junction with junction number

Motorway junction with limited interchange

Motorway under construction with proposed opening date where known

Trunk road with service area

Main road

Roundabout or multiple level junction

Secondary road

Road under construction

Toll   Road tunnel

Narrow road with passing places

Other tarred road   Other minor road

Gradient 1 in 7 and steeper

Distances in miles between markers

The representation of a road is no evidence of the existence of a right of way

PRIMARY ROUTES

These form a national network of recommended through routes which complement the motorway system. Selected places of major traffic importance are known as Primary Route Destinations and are shown thus YORK
Distances and directions to such destinations are repeated on traffic signs which, on primary routes, have a green background or, on motorways, have a blue background.
To continue on a primary route through or past a place which has appeared as a destination on previous signs, follow the directions to the next primary destination shown on the green-backed signs.

RAILWAYS

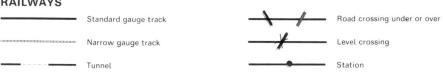

Standard gauge track

Narrow gauge track

Tunnel

Road crossing under or over

Level crossing

Station

WATER FEATURES

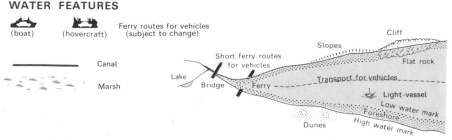

(boat)   (hovercraft)   Ferry routes for vehicles (subject to change)

Canal

Marsh

Lake   Bridge   Ferry

Short ferry routes for vehicles

Cliff

Slopes

Flat rock

Transport for vehicles

Light-vessel

Low water mark

Foreshore

High water mark

Dunes

ANTIQUITIES

✳ Native fortress   ⚔ Site of battle (with date)   ‧‧‧‧‧‧ Roman road (course of)   CANOVIUM ‧ Roman antiquity

Castle ‧   Other antiquities

𝔪   Ancient Monuments and Historic Buildings in the care of the Secretaries of State for the Environment, for Scotland and for Wales and that are open to the public.

BOUNDARIES

+ − + − + − + − National

− − − − − − − { County, Region or Islands Area

GENERAL FEATURES

 Buildings

 Wood

▲ Youth hostel

⊕ } Civil aerodrome { with Customs facilities

✦ } { without Customs facilities

⋏ Lighthouse (in use)   ⋏ Lighthouse (disused)

Ⓗ Heliport

𝄐 Windmill   Ⱦ Radio or TV mast

📞 Public telephone

📞 Motoring organisation telephone

+ Intersection, latitude & longitude at 30′ intervals (not shown where it confuses important detail)

TOURIST INFORMATION

✝ Abbey, Cathedral, Priory

🐟 Aquarium

⋀ Camp site

🚐 Caravan site

🏰 Castle

Cave

Country park

Craft centre

✿ Garden

▶ Golf course or links

🏠 Historic house

ℹ Information centre

🏎 Motor racing

🖼 Museum

❗ Nature or forest trail

🦆 Nature reserve

☆ Other tourist feature

✕ Picnic site

🚂 Preserved railway

🏃 Racecourse

⛷ Skiing

Viewpoint

Wildlife park

🐘 Zoo

WALKS, CYCLE & MOTOR TOURS
Applicable to all scales

 Start point of walk

➡ Route of walk

▬ Featured walk

 Start point of tour

➡ Route of tour

▬ Featured tour

■ Start point of mini-walk

FOLLOW THE COUNTRY CODE
Enjoy the countryside and respect its life and work

Guard against all risk of fire

Fasten all gates

Keep your dogs under close control

Keep to public paths across farmland

Leave livestock, crops and machinery alone

Use gates and stiles to cross fences, hedges and walls

Take your litter home

Help to keep all water clean

Protect wildlife, plants and trees

Take special care on country roads

Make no unnecessary noise

CONVENTIONAL SIGNS
1:25 000 or 2½ INCHES to 1 MILE

ROADS AND PATHS

Not necessarily rights of way

M I or A 6(M)	M I or A 6(M)	Motorway
A 31 (T)	A 31(T)	Trunk road
A 35	A 35	Main road
B 3074	B 3074	Secondary road
A 35	A 35	Dual carriageway

Narrow roads with passing places are annotated

Road generally more than 4m wide

Road generally less than 4m wide

Other road, drive or track

Unfenced roads and tracks are shown by pecked lines

Path

PUBLIC RIGHTS OF WAY

Public rights of way may not be evident on the ground

Public paths { Footpath / Bridleway }

Byway open to all traffic
Road used as a public path

The indication of a towpath in this book does not necessarily imply a public right of way

The representation of any other road, track or path is no evidence of the existence of a right of way

BOUNDARIES

— · — · — County (England and Wales)

— — — — District

—∘—∘—∘— London Borough

· · · · · · · Civil Parish (England)* Community (Wales)

— — — — — Constituency (County, Borough, Burgh or European Assembly)

Coincident boundaries are shown by the first appropriate symbol

*For Ordnance Survey purposes County Boundary is deemed to be the limit of the parish structure whether or not a parish area adjoins

RAILWAYS

Multiple track } Standard gauge
Single track

Narrow gauge

Siding

Cutting

Embankment

Tunnel

Road over & under

Level crossing; station

DANGER AREA

MOD ranges in the area
Danger!
Observe warning notices

Mountain Rescue Post

SYMBOLS

♦ Church	with tower	
♦ or	with spire	
+ chapel	without tower or spire	

⊠ ▲ Glasshouse; youth hostel

Bus or coach station

Lighthouse; lightship; beacon

△ Triangulation station

Triangulation point on { church or chapel / lighthouse, beacon / building; chimney }

Electricity transmission line
pylon   pole

VILLA   Roman antiquity (AD 43 to AD 420)

Castle   Other antiquities

⊹ Site of antiquity

✕ 1066   Site of battle (with date)

Gravel pit

Sand pit

Chalk pit, clay pit or quarry

Refuse or slag heap

Sloping wall

Water   Mud

Sand; sand & shingle

National Park or Forest Park Boundary

NT   National Trust always open

NT   National Trust opening restricted

FC   Forestry Commission

VEGETATION
Limits of vegetation are defined by positioning of the symbols but may be delineated also by pecks or dots

Coniferous trees

Non-coniferous trees

Coppice

Orchard

Scrub

Bracken, rough grassland
In some areas bracken (∂) and rough grassland (· · · · ·) are shown separately

Heath

Shown collectively as rough grassland on some sheets

Reeds

Marsh

Saltings

HEIGHTS AND ROCK FEATURES

50 ·
285 ·
Determined by { ground survey / air survey }

Surface heights are to the nearest metre above mean sea level. Heights shown close to a triangulation pillar refer to the station height at ground level and not necessarily to the summit

Vertical face

Loose rock   Boulders   Outcrop   Scree

75
60
50

Contours are at 5 metres vertical interval

ABBREVIATIONS
1:25 000 or 2½ INCHES to 1 MILE also 1:10 000/1:10 560 or 6 INCHES to 1 MILE

BP,BS	Boundary Post or Stone	P	Post Office	A,R	Telephone, AA or RAC
CH	Club House	Pol Sta	Police Station	TH	Town Hall
F V	Ferry Foot or Vehicle	PC	Public Convenience	Twr	Tower
FB	Foot Bridge	PH	Public House	W	Well
HO	House	Sch	School	Wd Pp	Wind Pump
MP,MS	Mile Post or Stone	Spr	Spring		
Mon	Monument	T	Telephone, public		

Abbreviations applicable only to 1:10 000/1:10 560 or 6 INCHES to 1 MILE

Ch	Church	GP	Guide Post	TCB	Telephone Call Box
F Sta	Fire Station	P	Pole or Post	TCP	Telephone Call Post
Fn	Fountain	S	Stone	Y	Youth Hostel

Maps and Mapping

Most early maps of the area covered by this guide were published on a county basis, and, if you wish to follow their development in detail, R. V. Tooley's *Maps and Map Makers* will be found most useful. The first significant county maps were produced by Christopher Saxton in the 1570s, the whole of England and Wales being covered in only six years. Although he did not cover the whole country, John Norden, working at the end of the sixteenth century, was the first map-maker to show roads. In 1611-12, John Speed, making use of Saxton's and Norden's pioneer work, produced his *Theatre of the Empire of Great Britaine*, adding excellent town plans, battle scenes, and magnificent coats of arms. The next great English map-maker was John Ogilby and, in 1675, he published *Britannia*, Volume I, in which all the roads of England and Wales were engraved on a scale of one inch to the mile, in a massive series of strip maps. From this time onwards, no map was published without roads, and, throughout the eighteenth century, steady progress was made in accuracy, if not always in the beauty of presentation.

The first Ordnance Survey maps came about as a result of Bonnie Prince Charlie's Jacobite rebellion of 1745. It was, however, in 1791, following the successful completion of the military survey of Scotland by General Roy that the Ordnance Survey was formally established. The threat of invasion by Napoleon in the early nineteenth century spurred on the demand for accurate and detailed mapping for military purposes, and, to meet this need, the first Ordnance Survey one-inch map, covering part of Essex, was published in 1805 in a single colour. This was the first numbered sheet in the First Series of one-inch maps.

Over the next seventy years, the one-inch map was extended to cover the whole of Great Britain. Reprints of some of the First Series maps, incorporating various later nineteenth-century amendments, have been published by David & Charles. The reprinted sheets covering most of our area are Numbers 12, 13, 16, and 17. The Ordnance Survey's one-inch maps evolved through a number of 'Series' and 'Editions' to the Seventh Series which was replaced in 1974 by the metric 1:50 000 scale Landranger Series. Between the First Series one-inch and the current Landranger maps, many changes in style, format, content, and purpose have taken place. Colour, for example, first appeared with the timid use of light brown for hill shading on the 1889 one-inch sheets. By 1892, as many as five colours were being used for this scale and, at one stage, the Seventh Series was being printed in no less than ten colours. Recent developments in 'process printing' — a technique in which four basic colours produce any required tint — are now used to produce Ordnance Survey Landranger and other maps series. Through the years, the one-inch Series has gradually turned away from its military origins and has developed to meet a wider user demand. The modern, detailed, full-colour Landranger maps at 1:50 000 scale incorporate Rights of Way and Tourist Information, and are much used for both leisure and business purposes. To compare the old and new approaches to changing demand, see the two map extracts of Harrogate on the following pages.

Modern Ordnance Survey Maps of the Area

The Yorkshire Dales and York are covered by Ordnance Survey 1:50 000 scale (1¼ inches to 1 mile) Landranger map sheets 91, 92, 98, 104, and 105. These all-purpose maps are packed full of information to help you explore the area. Viewpoints, picnic sites, places of interest, caravan and camping sites are shown, as is public rights of way information such as footpaths and bridleways.

To examine the Yorkshire Dales in more detail and especially if you are planning walks, Ordnance Survey Outdoor Leisure Maps at 1:25 000 (2½ inches to 1 mile) are ideal. Three Outdoor Leisure Maps cover the main Yorkshire Dales National Park area as follows:

Sheet 2 — Yorkshire Dales - Western Area
Sheet 10 — Yorkshire Dales - Southern Area
Sheet 30 — Yorkhire Dales - North and
Central Area

To look at the area surrounding the Yorkshire Dales, Ordnance Survey 1:250 000 scale (1 inch to 4 miles) will prove most useful; Sheet 5 Northern England, and Sheet 6 East Midlands and Yorkshire are relevant.

To place the area in an historical context, the following Ordnance Historical Maps and Guides will be useful: Ancient Britain, Roman Britain, Britain before the Norman Conquest. There are also special historical maps of York; Roman and Anglian York, Viking and Medieval York.

Ordnance Survey maps are available from officially appointed agents (see addresses of local agents below) and most booksellers and stationers.

Thomas C Godfrey Ltd
32 Stonegate
York
YO1 2AP
Tel 0904 624531

F B Jasper and Son Ltd
14 Oxford Street
Harrogate
HG1 1PU
Tel 0423 503998

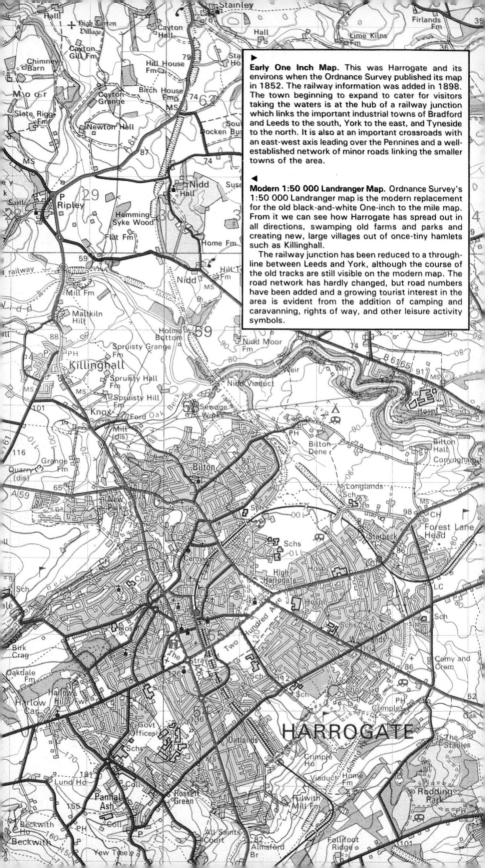

Early One Inch Map. This was Harrogate and its environs when the Ordnance Survey published its map in 1852. The railway information was added in 1898. The town beginning to expand to cater for visitors taking the waters is at the hub of a railway junction which links the important industrial towns of Bradford and Leeds to the south, York to the east, and Tyneside to the north. It is also at an important crossroads with an east-west axis leading over the Pennines and a well-established network of minor roads linking the smaller towns of the area.

Modern 1:50 000 Landranger Map. Ordnance Survey's 1:50 000 Landranger map is the modern replacement for the old black-and-white One-inch to the mile map. From it we can see how Harrogate has spread out in all directions, swamping old farms and parks and creating new, large villages out of once-tiny hamlets such as Killinghall.

The railway junction has been reduced to a through-line between Leeds and York, although the course of the old tracks are still visible on the modern map. The road network has hardly changed, but road numbers have been added and a growing tourist interest in the area is evident from the addition of camping and caravanning, rights of way, and other leisure activity symbols.

Index

The first set of numbers refers to pages; page numbers in *italics* refer to illustrations

SUBJECT	PAGE NO.	MAP NO. MAP REF.
Adam, Robert	65	
Agnes Grey	17	
Ailesbury, Earl of	45	
Aire, River	47, 89	
Airedale	57, 63	
Aislabie, William	71	
All Creatures Great and Small	33	
Appersett	11, 32	**98** SD 86-91
Appleby	18	
Appletreewick	32, 40	**98** SE 05-60
Arkengarthdale	11, *14*, 33, 61, *68*, 95	
Arncliffe	32, 64, 89, 126	**98** SD 93-71
Arkle Beck	95	
Ash Fell	98	
Askrigg	32-3, 73, 96	**98** SD 94-91
Attermire Cave	61	
Austwick	33	**98** SD 76-68
Assembly Rooms, York	80	**98** SE 00-88
Aysgarth	8, 9, 13, 15, 23, 33-4, 76, 77, 94-5	
Bain, River	34, 94, 120, 121	
Bainbridge	34, 94, 120, *120*, 121	**98** SD 93-90
Baliol, Guy and Bernard de	35	
Baliol, John	36	
Balliol College, Oxford	36	
Bank Newton	*15*, 34, 45, 88	**103** SD 91-53
Barben Beck	54	
Barbon	34	**97** SD 62-82
Barbon Beck	34	
Barden Bridge	22, 108	
Barden Tower	18, *18*, *34*, 35, 37, 86, 87, 89, 108	**104** SE 05-57
Barnard Castle	13, 35-6, *36*, 100, 101	**92** NZ 05-16
Barningham	36, 100,	**92** NZ 08-10
Barningham Park	36	
Barnoldswick	36	**103** SD 87-46
Batty Green	117	
Batty Moss Viaduct *see* Ribblehead		
Baugh Fell	50, 99	
Beamsley	37	
Beamsley Hospital	37, 87	
Beamsley Moor	87	
Becket, Thomas à	61	
Beck Foot	98	
Bedale	33	
Bedlam	102	
Beeching, Dr Richard	13	
Belah, River	99	
Bewerley	37	**99** SE 15-65
Bingley	104	
Bishop Wilfrid	71	
birds	25-7	
Birstwith	87	
Bishopdale	8, 43, 65, 76, 96	
Bloodaxe, Erik	81	
Blubberhouses	37, 87	**104** SE 17-55
Blubberhouses Moor	87	
Bolton Abbey	22, 46, 87, 108	**104** SE 07-54
Bolton Castle	40, 41, 62, 125	
Bolton Hall	37, 78, 96, 124	
Bolton Priory	12, *12*, 32, 37, *37*, 57, 72, 86, 90	
Bolton, Third Duke of	79	
Booze	61	
Boroughbridge	102, 103	
Bouthwaite	90	
Bowes	37-8, *37*, 39, 100, 130, 131	**92** NY 99-13
Bowes, George	36	
Bowes Museum	36, *36*	
Bowland, Forest of	88	
Braithwaite Hall	45, 91	
Bramhope Tunnel	66	
Branwell, Maria	16	
Brigflatts	72-3, 93	
Brignall Banks	*24*, 38, 100	**92** NZ 05-11
Brimham House	38	
Brimham Rocks	8, 18, 38, 102, 103	**99** SE 21-65
Brontë, Branwell	16	
Brontë, Charlotte	87, 105	
Brontë family	16-17, 43, 92, 104-5	
Brontë Parsonage Museum	105	
Brontë, Rev. Patrick	16, 105	
Brough	18, 38-9, *38*, 99	**91** NY 79-14
Brough Sowerby	99	
Brougham Castle	18	
Brown, Capability	22, 70	
Buckden	39, 126	**98** SD 94-77
Burley in Wharfedale	39	**104** SE 16-46
Burley Woodhead	104	
Burn, River	90	
Burnsall	32, 39-40, *39*, 54, 86	**98** SE 03-61
Burnt Yates	87, 102	

SUBJECT	PAGE NO.	MAP NO. MAP REF.
Burtersett 94		
Burton in Lonsdale 40		97 SD 65-72
Butler, Samuel 69		
Butter Tubs Pass 40, *40*, 78, 95		
Caldwell 101		
Cam Beck 23		
Carleton 105		
Carlton 40-1, 91		99 SE 06-84
Carperby 41, 95		98 SE 00-89
Casterton 41, 93		97 SD 62-79
Castle Bolton 34, 41, 95		
Castle Dykes 9		
Castle Museum, York 81		
Catterick Garrison 41		99 SE 18-97
Catterick village		41
Cautley Spout 41, *41*, *42*, 99		
Cavendish, Frederick Charles 109		
Chapel-le-Dale 10, 41-2, 79, 92, 116		98 SD 74-77
Charlie, Bonny Prince 63, 72		
Chippendale, Thomas 66		
Church Brough *38*, 42, 99		
Clapdale Woods 42		
Clapham 13, 33, 42, *106*		98 SD 74-69
Clapham Beck 42		
Clifford, Lady Anne 18, 34, 35, 37, 39, 67, 73, 108		
Clifford, Tenth Lord Henry 35		
Clifford Tower, York 81		
Clough, River 48, *48*		
Cogden Gill 50		
Colt Park Wood 20		
Conistone 42, 91		98 SD 98-67
Constable Burton Hall 42		99 SE 16-91
Constantine the Great 10		
Constantine, Henry 41		
Corpse Way 46-7, 50, *50*, 97, 126		
Countersett 11, 43, 94, 120, 121		98 SD 91-87
Cover, River 43, 70		
Coverdale 33, 40-1, 43, 55, 56, 76, 90, 91		
Coverham 43, 44, 56		99 SE 10-86
Coverham Abbey 43, 56, 91		
Coverham Bridge 91		
Cowan Bridge 16, 41, 43, 92		97 SD 64-77
Cow and Calf rocks 56, 104		
Cowgill 92		
Cowper Gill 109		
Craven Moor 86		
Craven, Sir William 32, 40		
Cray 43, 96, 127		98 SD 94-79
Cray Gill 126		
Crimple viaduct *51*		
Cromwell, Oliver 59, 61		
Cubeck 94		
Cullingworth 105		
Culloden Tower 69		
Cumberland, George, Earl of 18, 37		
Cumberland, Margaret, Countess of 37		
Dalesman, The 42		
Dales Way 17, 108, 113, 119, 126		
Dalton 101		
Danny Bridge *48*		
Dark Ages 10		
Dee, River 93, 118, 119		
Deepdale Beck 119		
Defoe, Daniel 16, 71		
Dent 44, 92, 119, *119*		98 SD 70-86
Dentdale 92		
Dent Station 92		
Devil's Arrows, The 103		
Dibb, River 86		
Dickens, Charles 36, 38, 85, 130		
Dodd Fell 25		
Doe, River 56		
Dotheboys Hall 36, 38, 130		
Dropping Well 60		
Druid's Temple 61		
Duerley Beck 48		
drystone walls 22		
Earby 44		103 SD 90-46
Earby Mines Research Group 44		
Easby 44-5, *44*, 101		92 NZ 18-00
Easby Abbey 44-5, 48		
Eastby 89		
East Marton 45		103 SD 90-50
East Witton 45, *45*, 90		99 SE 14-86
Eden, River 59, 65, 67, *67*, 99, 128		
Edward II 18		
Egglestone Abbey 46, *46*		92 NZ 06-15
Ellerton Abbey 97		
Ellingstring 90		
Elslack Moor 105		
Embsay 13, 46, 89		104 SE 01-53

INDEX

SUBJECT	PAGE NO.	MAP NO.	MAP REF.

Embsay Moor 46
Eshton 46   103 SD 93-56
Eshton Hall 46
Eskeleth 95
Ewbank Scar 129

Farrer, Reginald 42
Feetham and Low
   Row 46-7, 50, 97   98 SD 98-98
Fewston 36, 37, 47, 86   104 SE 19-54
Fitzrobert, Ranulf 43
Forcett Park 101
Forest of Knaresborough 60,
   76   104 SE 35-57
Foss, River 81
Foster Beck Mill 66, *66*, 90
Fountains Abbey 12, 37, 47,
   47, 57, 90, 102, 103
Fountains Fell 12, 47, 112
Fox, George 72
Freeholders Wood 23, 34
Fremington Edge 64, *68*

Gaping Gill 42
Gargrave 46, 47-8, 88   103 SD 93-54
Garibaldi 34
Garsdale 13, 48, *48*   98 SD 74-89
Garsdale Head 48, *48*, 92   98 SD 78-92
Garsdale Station 92
Gaunt, Elizabeth 67
Gayle 48, 54, 96   98 SD 87-89
Gayle Moor 92
Gayles 101
Georgian Theatre,
   Richmond 69
Giggleswick 48, *48*, 73   98 SD 81-64
Giggleswick Scar 48
Gilling West 101
Gilmonby 131
Gilmonby Moor 130
Glasshouses 87
God's Bridge 48, *49*   92 NY 95-12
Gordale Bridge 111
Gordale Scar 8, 16, 48, 63,
   75, 110, *110*, 111
Gouthwaite Reservoir 26, 48,
   67, *67*, 90, *90*, 114
Grassington 9, 11, 13, 14,
   48-9, 57, 62, 86, 89, 90, 91,
   107, 112, 112, 113   98 SE 00-64
Great Musgrave 99
Green Howards Museum,
   Richmond 69
Greenhow Hill 49, 86   99 SE 11-64

Greta Bridge 38, 49, 100   92 NZ 08-13
Greta, River 24, 37, 38, 40,
   48, 49, *49*, 56, 72, 92,
   100, 130, 131
Grey Gill 111
Grinton 46, 49-50, *50*, 95, 97   98 SE 04-98
Grisedale 50   98 SD 77-93
Guildhall, York 84
Gunnerside 50, 97   98 SD 95-98
Gunnerside Gill 50, *50*, *96*   98 SD 87-89

Halton Gill 51, 89   98 SD 88-76
Hardraw 8, 51, *51*   98 SD 86-91
Harlow Car Gardens 53
Harrogate 51-3, *53*, 102,
   103   104 SE 30-55
Hartlington 54   98 SE 03-61
Haw Park Hill 46
Hawes 13, 15, 25, 32, 40, 48,
   54, *54*, 77, 92, 94, 95, 96,
   125
Haworth 13, 16-17, *16*, *17*,
   104, 105
Healey 90
Hebden 49, 55, 90, 112, 113   98 SE 02-63
Hebden Beck 90
Hebden Brook 55
Hebden Moor 89
Hellifield 55   103 SD 85-56
Henry III 66
Henry IV 60
Henry VII 85
Henry VIII 12, 37, 57, 80
Herriot, James 32, 33, 41, 96
Hewitt, Rev. Matthew 78
High Birkwith 23
Horsehouse 55   98 SE 04-81
Horton in Ribblesdale 23, 55   98 SD 80-72
Hotspur, Harry 75
How Stean 63, 114, *114*
Howgill Fells 41, 99
Hubberholme 19, 43, 55, *55*,
   96, 126, 127   98 SD 92-78
Huby, Marmaduke 37
Hudson, George 15, 84
Hunters Stone 56, 91

Ilkley 56, 104   104 SE 12-47
Ilkley Moor 8, 104
Ingilby, Sir William
   Amcotts 70
Ingleborough 42, 56, 77, 92,
   116, *117*
Ingleborough Cave 42, *43*

SUBJECT	PAGE NO.	MAP NO. MAP REF.
Ingleton 13, *27*, 56, *56*, 79, 92		
Ivelet 56, *56*, 97		98 SD 93-98
James I 71		
Jane Eyre 16, 41, 43, 105		
Janet's Foss 63, 111		
Jefferies, Judge 67		
Jervaulx Abbey 12, 13, 50, 56-7, *57*, 78, 90		99 SE 17-85
Jervaulx Hall 57		
John of Gaunt 61		
Jorvik Viking Centre 11, 81		
Kean, Edmund 49		
Keighley 13, 105		
Keighley & Worth Valley Railway 13, 105		
Keld 57, 95, 122, *122*, 123		92 NY 89-01
Kettlewell 56, 57, 90, 91		98 SD 97-72
Kildwick 57		104 SE 01-46
Killinghall 102		
Kilnsey 12, 42, 57, 89		98 SD 97-67
Kilnsey Crag 8, 57, 91		
Kilnsey Moor *57*		
Kingsley, Charles 32		
Kirby Hill 101		
Kirk Deighton 103		
Kirkby Lonsdale 9, 16, 58, 92, 93		97 SD 61-78
Kirkby Malham 58-9, *59*, 89		98 SD 89-61
Kirkby Stephen 13, 59, *59*, 98, 99, 128, *128*		91 NY 77-08
Kisdon Force 57, 95, 122, 123		
Knaresborough 52, 59-61, 75, 76, 102, 103		
Ladthwaite Beck 129		
lakes and rivers 24-5		
Laneshaw Bridge 105		
Langcliffe 61		98 SD 82-65
Langcliffe Scar 61		
Langstrothdale 39, 66, 79, 126		98 SD 90-79
Langthorpe 103		
Langthwaite 33, 61, *61*, 95		92 NZ 00-02
lead mining 14, 44, 47, 49, 50, 57, 61, 66, 68, 76, 95, 107, 112, *112*		
Leck Beck 43, 92		
Leeds and Liverpool Canal 15, *15*, 34, 36, 45, 48, 57, 73, 74-5, 88, *89*		
Leeds-Harrogate railway line *51*		
Leeds and Thirsk Railway 66		
Leighton 61		99 SE 16-79
Leighton Reservoir 90		
Leyburn 3 3, 61-2, *61*, 96, 97		99 SE 11-90
Leyburn to Redmire railway line 13		
Lindley Wood Reservoir 37		
Linton 49, 62		98 SD 99-62
Linton Falls 49, 113		
Little Ribston 103		
Littondale 32, 51, 89		
Lofthouse 62-3, *62*, 72, 90, 114, 115		99 SE 10-73
London North Western Railway 15		
Long Gill Wood 23		
Long Preston 62, 88		103 SD 83-58
Lothersdale 105		
Low Gill 13		
Low Row *see* Feetham		
Lune, River 25, 41, 58, 65, 93, 98		
Malham 10, 11, 16, 19, *20*, 46, 47, 63-4, 75, 88, 89, 110, 111		98 SD 90-63
Malham Beck 89		
Malham Cove 8, 9, 57, 63, *63*, 64, 89, 110, 127		
Malham Tarn 10, 12, 25, 64		
mammals 27		
Market Brough 38, 64		
Marrick 64		99 SE 07-98
Marrick Priory 97		
Marske 64		92 SZ 10-00
Mary, Queen of Scots 41, 62		
Masham 64-5, *64*		99 SE 22-80
Mastiles Gate *57*		
Mastiles Lane 12		
Melmerby Moor 124		
Menston 104		
Merchant Adventurers Hall, York 81		
Metcalf, Blind Jack 61, 75		
Micklethwaite 104		
Middleham 65		99 SE 12-87
Middleham Low Moor *65*		
Middlesmoor 65, 114		99 SE 09-74
Midland Railway 15, 46		

SUBJECT	PAGE NO.	MAP NO. MAP REF.
Mill Gill 33		
Minster Library, York 80		
Moorcock Inn 48, 92		
Mossdale 92		
Mother Shipton's Cave 60		
Muker 11, 50, 65, 78, 96, 122		**98** SD 90-97
Nateby 65, 99, 128, 129		**91** NY 77-06
National Railway Museum 15, 84		
National Trust 38, 41, 47, 64, 91, 103		
Newbiggin 65, 76, 96		**98** SD 99-85
Newbiggin on Lune 65, 98		**91** NY 70-05
Newby Hall 65, 103		**99** SE 34-67
Newsham 101		
New York 87		
Nicholas Nickleby 36, 38, 85, 130		
Nicholls, Rev. Arthur 17		
Nidd, River 59-60, 66, 67, 86, 87, 90, 102, 103		
Nidd Valley Light Railway 63		
Nidderdale 13, 22, *25*, 38, 47, 62, *62*, 65, 67, 72, 90, 114		
Nidderdale Museum 66		
Nidderdale Way 114		
Norber boulders *20*, 33		
Norber Hill 33		
North Stainmore 65		**92** NY 83-15
Norton, Francis 72		
Norton Tower 72		
Otley 66		**104** SE 20-45
Oughtershaw 66, 96		**98** SD 87-81
Oughtershaw Beck 66		
Ouse, River 81, 84		
Oxenhope 13		
Parcevall Hall 66, 75, 89		
Pateley Bridge 37, 66, 72, 86, 87, 90		**99** SE 15-65
Pendle Hill 110		
Pendragon Castle 66-7, *67*, *98*, 99		
Pennine Way 17, 23, 45, 48, 55, 70, 78, 95, 110, 111, 122, 123, 130, 131		
Pen-y-ghent 55, 77, 89, 112		
Plumpton Rocks 67, 103		**104** SE 35-53
Ponden Hill 105		
Ponden Reservoir 105		

SUBJECT	PAGE NO.	MAP NO. MAP REF.
Preston-under-Scar 125		
Prison and Police Museum, Ripon 71-2		
Professor, The 17		
Railway Children, The 13		
railways in the Dales 13		
Ramsgill 66, 67, *67*, 90		**99** SE 11-71
Randolph, Ralph Fitz 75		
Ravenstonedale 67, 98, 99		**91** NY 72-04
Rawthey, River 93,99		
Redmire 68, 124		**98** SE 04-91
Redmire Force 68		
Reeth 33, *68*, 68		**98** SE 03-99
Ribble, River 48, 73, 75-6, 88		
Ribblehead viaduct 13, 42, 68, 92, 116		
Richard II 36, 41, 84		
Richard III 65, 85		
Richmond, 11, *11*, 44, 69, *69*, 97, 101		**92** NZ 17-01
Rievaulx Abbey 85		
Ripley 70, *70*, 102		**99** SE 28-60
Ripley, Hugh 71		
Ripon 70-2, *71*, 102, 103		**99** SE 31-71
Ripon Canal 72, 103		
Roalbus, Constable of Richmond 45		
Robinson Richard 43, 120		
Robinson, Sir Thomas 72		
Rokeby 38, 72		
Rokeby Park 49, 72		**92** NZ 08-14
Rokeby Venus, The 72		
Royal Baths and Assembly Rooms, Harrogate 52		
Royal Pump Room Museum, Harrogate 52		
Rufus, Alan 69		
Ruskin, John 58		
Rylstone 72		**103** SD 96-58
Rylstone Fell 110		
Sawley 103		
Scandal beck 67		
Scargill 38, 100		
Scar House Reservoir 13, 26, 114		**98/99** SD 06-76
Stosthrop Moor 89		
Scott, Sir Walter 38, 72		
Scrope, Lord 41		
Sedbergh 13, 48, 72-3, 92, *92*, 93, 98, 99		**97/98** SD 65-92
Sedgwick, Adam 44, 119		

SUBJECT	PAGE NO.	MAP NO. MAP REF.	SUBJECT	PAGE NO.	MAP NO. MAP REF.
Semer Water	16, 25, 34, 43, 72, *73*, 94, 120, 121	**98** SD 92-87	Thompson, Robert	55	
Settle	9, 12, 48, 55, 73, *73*, 88, 89	**98** SD 81-63	Thornton Force	*8*	
			Thornton Rust	77, 94	**98** SD 97-88
Settle and Carlisle Railway	13, 15, 42, 48, 55, 73, 92, 116, 128		Three Peaks, The	21, 77, 92	
			Threshfield	77-8, *77*, 89	
			Thruscross Reservoir	37	
Shap Fell	15		Thwaite	78, 95	**98** SD 89-98
Shirley	17, 104, 105		Timble	87	
Skell, River	47, 70, 72, 103		Top Withins	105	
Skelton	103		Treasurer's House York	80	
Skipton	11, 13, 18, 35, 46, 49, 55, 73-5, *74*, 88, 89, *89*, 91, 104, 105	**103** SD 98-51	Trollers Gill	75, 89	
			Turner, J M W	16	
			Turpin, Dick	81	
Skirfare, River	32		Twiss, River	56	
Skyreholme	**75**	**99** SE 06-60			
Sleightholme Beck	130, 131		Ulshaw Bridge	45	
			Uplands	19-21	
Slingsby, William	52		Upper Dales Folk Museum	54, *54*	
Spence, Sir Basil	85				
Spennithorne	45, 75	**99** SE 13-89	Upper Wharfedale Museum	49, *49*	
Spofforth	75, 103	**104** SE 36-51			
Stainforth	75-6	**98** SD 82-67	Ure, River	27, 32, 34, 54, 56, 62, 65, 68, 70-1, 95, 96, 103, 124	
Stainforth Force	76				
Stanbury	105				
Stanwick Camp	101				
Starbotton	76	**98** SD 95-74			
Stean	114		Vanbrugh, Sir John	62	
Stean Gill	63		valleys	23-4	
Stonesdale Moor	76		Velasquez	72	
Straw beck	65, 122		Victoria Cave	9, 61	
Strid	22, 37, *86*, 87, 108-9		*Villette*	17	
Studley Roger	47, 76, 103				
Studley Royal	47, 76, 103				
Stump Cross Caverns	76, 76, 86	**99** SE 08-63	Wain Wath Force	95	
			Wakeman	71	
Swainby	43		Walden Beck	79	
Swale, River	49, 56, *56*, 65, 68, 95, 97, 122, *122*		Warwick the Kingmaker	36	
			Washburn valley	25, *36*, 37	
Swaledale	14, 23, *23*, 33, 43, 50, 57, 64, 97		*Water Babies, The*	32	
			waterfalls	8	
Swaledale Folk Museum	95		Watermill Inn *see* Foster Beck Mill		
Swarcliffe Hall	87		Wath	11	
Swinner Gill	122, 123		Wensley	13, 78, *78*, 79, 96, 124, 125	**99** SE 09-89
Swinithwaite	76, 96	**98** SE 04-89			
Swinsty Reservoir	37, 86		Wensleydale	8, 16, 22, 33, 34, 41, 43, 54, 79, 92, 94, 95, 120, 124, 125	
Tan Hill	76, 95, *95*	**91** NY 90-07	Wensleydale cheese	54, 57, 78	
Tebay	98				
Tees, River	35, 46, 49, 100, 101		West Burton	79, 96	**98** SE 01-86
			West New House	13, 65, 96	
Thoralby	76-7, *76*	**98** SE 00-86			
Theakstons Brewery	*64*, 65		West Stonesdale	95	
			West Witton	79, 96	**98/99** SE 06-88

INDEX

SUBJECT	PAGE NO.	MAP NO. MAP REF.
Wetherby	102, 103	
Wharfe, River	25, 27, 37, 37, 39, 39, 54, 55, 66, 86, 89, 91, 103, 108, 112, 113, 126	
Wharfedale	16, 22, 32, 39, 42, 56, 57, 86, 90, 104, 112, 127	
Wharton Fell	99	
Wharton Hall	65, 128	
Whaw	95	
Whernside	42, 77, 116	
White Doe of Rylstone	72	
White Scar Caves	56, 79, 92	**98** SD 71-74
Whitfield Gill Force	23, 33	
Widdale	92	
Widdale Beck	32	
Wild Boar Fell	50	
William the Conqueror	35, 81	
Winterscales beck	117	
Winton	101	
woodland	22-3	
Wordsworth, William	72	
Wuthering Heights	17, 104, 105	
Wycoller	105	
Yockenthwaite	79, 79, 96, 126	**98** SD 90-79
Yockenthwaite stone circle	127	
York	10, 11, 12, 15, 47, 66, 75, 80-5, 103	**105** SE 59-51
York Abbey	58	
York Castle Museum	80	
York Minster	12, 15, 38, 42, 80, 85	
Yorkshire Carriage Museum	34	
Yorkshire County Cricket Club	36	
Yorkshire Dales Cycle Way	125	
Yorkshire Dales Lead-mining Museum	44	
Yorkshire Dales National Park	18, 21, 23, 24, 27, 42, 48, 54, 64, 86, 90, 95, 110	
Yorkshire Dales Railway	13, 46, 89	
Yorkshire Water	26, 72	